FOR THE LOVE OF A CASTLE

THE BIOGRAPHY OF CASTLE FARMS, CHARLEVOIX, MICHIGAN

❧

LINDA MUELLER

AND

KATHLEEN IRENE PATERKA

5052 M-66 NORTH
CHARLEVOIX, MICHIGAN 49720
PHONE: 231-237-0884
FAX: 231-237-0994
WWW.CASTLEFARMS.COM

For the Love of a Castle was researched, written and edited by Linda Mueller and Kathleen Irene Paterka for Castle Farms. Published by Harbor House Publishers, Inc. Manufactured in the United States of America. Printed in Michigan. Castle Farms and Harbor House Publishers, Inc. cannot guarantee the accuracy of the information presented here or be held accountable for any omissions or errors. Please report any corrections to Castle Farms.

ISBN 1-58241-448-3

Harbor House Publishers, Inc. | 221 Water Street, Boyne City, MI 49712 | 800-491-1760   fax: 866-906-3392 | www.harborhouse.com   harbor@harborhouse.com

DEDICATION

---✦---

This book is dedicated to Albert and Anna Loeb for their vision and love of castles
and to my husband, Richard Mueller, Jr., who made my dreams of a castle come true.

Devoted People Serving God by Preserving and Developing a

World-Class Historic Property to Benefit Individuals,

Families and the Charlevoix Community.

Castle Farms' Mission Statement enjoys a prominent spot in both the Main Office and Welcome Center.
It serves as a reminder of Linda Mueller's hope and vision for The Castle: to benefit the 50,000 individuals
who visit each year, the employees who are committed to providing World-Class Friendly Service to everyone
who enters the gates, and to be a blessing to the Charlevoix Community by bringing visitors to the area.

SPECIAL THANKS

This book would not have been possible without the collaborative efforts of many people who shared their knowledge with us in researching this book. Special thanks to Richard Mueller, Jr., Val Mueller, Anora Ruehle O'Connor, Peggy Kusina, Kevin Pearsall, David Ruehle, Suzanne Goodwin, George Lasater, Adele Forbrig, Virginia Lepman, Marsha Braun, Laurie Keller, Cyndi Urban, Joan DeBlock, Lynn Saunders, Larry Shawn, and Michelle Cortright and her wonderful team at Harbor House Publishers.

Kathleen Irene Paterka, a resident of Charlevoix, Michigan, shares Linda Mueller's passion for all things royal, especially the majestic stone towers of Castle Farms. Kathleen is the author of six novels. For more information, visit her website at www.kathleenirenepaterka.com.

THE CASTLE

Knight's Castle

Carriage Hall

Knight's Tower

1918 Museum/ Blacksmith Shop

Round Office

Cheese Box

King's Towers

West Garden Room

King's Castle

Queen's Tavern

King's Towers

Queen's Castle

East Garden Room

King's Great Hall (up)

King's Gallery (down)

Gift Shop/ Welcome Center

CONTENTS

❧

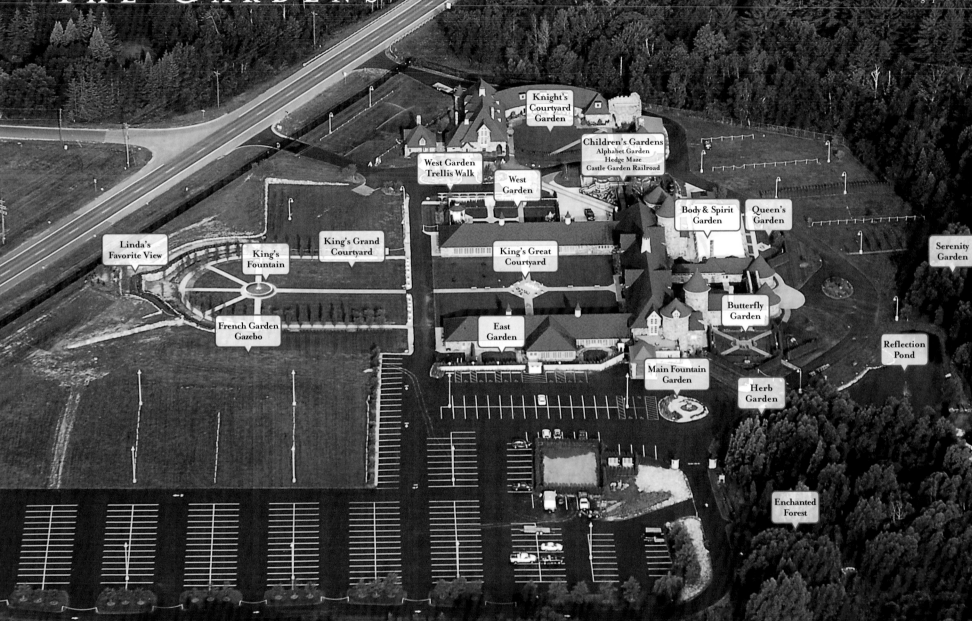

THE GARDENS

Photographed in 2010

Knight's Courtyard Garden

Children's Gardens
Alphabet Garden
Hedge Maze
Castle Garden Railroad

West Garden Trellis Walk

West Garden

Body & Spirit Garden

Queen's Garden

Serenity Garden

Linda's Favorite View

King's Grand Courtyard

King's Fountain

King's Great Courtyard

Butterfly Garden

Reflection Pond

French Garden Gazebo

East Garden

Main Fountain Garden

Herb Garden

Enchanted Forest

WELCOME TO THE CASTLE

Linda and husband,
Richard Mueller, Jr.

You may have looked up Castle Farms on the Internet and used your GPS to find us. Or you may have just been driving along a winding country road and spotted The Castle as if by magic. However you found your way here, Castle Farms has a charming habit of transporting visitors to different times and places where life slows down and surprises are around every corner.

You just might imagine yourself in 17th century France at a Renaissance castle surrounded with formal gardens. You might be taken back to 1918 when the United States was fighting in the War to End All Wars. You might revisit your childhood enjoying model trains and antique toys.

I hope you feel the peacefulness of the formal gardens, the playfulness of the children's gardens and outdoor trains, the natural wildness of the Enchanted Forest, the massiveness of boulders in the gardens and huge stone buildings, and the challenge of navigating through corridors, around multiple wings, and in and out of a complex of wonderful architecture.

I hope your imagination has a chance to blossom while you are here. Take some dreams home with you, and right away, plan your next adventure.

Welcome to Castle Farms!

Linda Mueller, *the Perpetual Dreamer*
Owner, Castle Farms

Enjoy quotes throughout the book in Linda Mueller's own words as she speaks from the heart on the Castle Farms experience.

TOP: *Loeb Farms in the early 1920s.*

BOTTOM: *Castle Farms, 2009.*

Photo credit: Karen Fordos & Domagalski Photography

HISTORY

Chicago residents remember June 1917 as being one of the coolest, rainiest months on record. But the cold weather couldn't dampen Albert Loeb's spirits. The wealthy entrepreneur and acting President of Sears Roebuck Company had just received good news from his attorney. Mr. Loeb's bid to purchase a tract of Northern Michigan property had been accepted, and he was now the proud owner of eight hundred acres of prime lakefront property located near the renowned summer resort community of Charlevoix. Soon after, the Loeb property grew to nearly 1800 acres. Mr. Loeb's vision of a country home and estate on the south shore of Lake Charlevoix would become a reality.

FOR THE LOVE OF A CASTLE

In 1917, with the United States having just been drawn into the fierce battle of World War I, the Charlevoix community longed for good news. When word began to circulate around the small summer resort town that a wealthy Chicago entrepreneur by the name of Albert Loeb had purchased a considerable amount of Northern Michigan land, residents immediately knew they had cause to celebrate.

A self-made man, Mr. Loeb understood the value of a dollar. He had worked his way through college, and over time, became a successful Chicago attorney. But a chance encounter with two individuals named Sears and Roebuck led Mr. Loeb to devote himself to the corporate world. Success inevitably followed. By 1917, he held a position in senior

Loeb Farms under construction, 1918.

management with Sears Roebuck Company. During WWI, he was called to serve as acting President of the corporation.

Albert Loeb had a particular fondness for the architecture of the Renaissance castles found throughout the French countryside. He found their distinctive Romanesque and Gothic arches, decorative turrets, ancient stone crenellations, and sweeping galleries pleasing to the eye. When the time came to draw up plans for his Charlevoix country estate, Mr. Loeb chose Arthur Heun, a renowned Chicago architect who had designed the Loeb family home in the exclusive area of Kenwood, Illinois.

Heun quickly got to work designing the Loeb's new home, which would be built high upon a bluff overlooking Lake Charlevoix. The final plans featured a palatial residence fit for a king. Known as "The Big House", it would become the summer residence of Mr. Loeb, his wife Anna, and their four sons. Heun was also commissioned to draw

up plans for a farm complex, to be modeled after the stone farms found in Normandy, France. Mr. Loeb envisioned a working dairy farm, with barns large enough to hold more than two hundred head of dairy cows and equipment to showcase modern technological advances in farming.

BUILDING BEGINS

Work commenced on "The Big House" in 1917. R.F. Sloan, Engineer for the City of Charlevoix, tendered his resignation with the City in July to take the position of construction manager. Native fieldstone from around the region was transported to the site, where thirty five skilled stone masons and local men labored to bring Heun's plans

> "The Castle Farms buildings were started less than 40 years after Neuschwanstein Castle in Germany was completed. They have very little in common except for round towers and steep roof lines because the building sites and purposes were so different. But Albert Loeb and King Ludwig both had a deep love of castles, romantic design, and quality craftsmanship. And they both died only a few years after the castles were in use. How sad."

1917

JUNE – Albert Loeb purchases nearly 1800 acres of property in Northern Michigan for summer residence and Loeb Farms complex

SUMMER – Architect Arthur Heun of Chicago commissioned by Albert Loeb to draw up architectural plans

R. F. Sloan, former Charlevoix City Engineer, is hired to serve as Construction Foreman

1918

Work commences on Loeb summer residence and barn complex

Livestock purchased, Loeb Farms opens for business as working model dairy farm

1919

Loeb Farms opens grounds to visitors (The Cheese Box, Sunday afternoon baseball games)

1920

Loeb cattle shown at National Dairy Show in Chicago, winning the two-year herd national acclaim

1922

Klorain Marion Finderne, a pedigree Holstein-Friesian dairy cow, produces thirty five thousand pounds of milk per year

1924

OCTOBER – Albert Loeb dies of a massive heart attack

FALL – Ernest Loeb, second son of Albert and Anna Loeb, takes over as Farm Manager of Loeb Farms

1927

Loeb Family makes decision to close Loeb Farms

FALL – Public auction of Loeb Farms livestock and equipment

Albert Loeb's famous cow Marion. Loeb Farms was a modern farm and one of the first in Michigan to use Tubercular testing. The farm included a cheese factory and delivered milk, cheese, butter, poultry and flowers in the Charlevoix area twice daily.

to life. Local residents watched with keen interest as work also began on the barns. Construction was a painstaking process. Eventually the buildings would include horse stables, a carriage hall, blacksmith shop, ice house, Farm Manager's office, a 'drive-by' summer shop which sold dairy products (dubbed The Cheese Box), as well as impressive dairy barns with stanchions for cattle and a dormitory for farm workers who would live onsite. Within two years, the entire construction project was completed. As Albert and Anna Loeb peacefully settled down with their family to enjoy their new summer residence, the nearby farm opened for business.

LIFE ON LOEB FARMS

Mr. Loeb's vision of a working dairy farm flourished. Loeb Farms—as it came to be known—eventually employed more than ninety people in its daily operations, making it the largest employer in Charlevoix County. A full-time vet-erinarian lived on site. Men lucky enough to garner a position working at the farm considered themselves fortunate. Housing was available for single men, with one wing of the dairy barn (known as "The Club") featuring card tables and modern shower baths. Mr. Loeb made every attempt to ensure his employees were provided with the best of modern-day conveniences.

His vision for excellence extended to the farm as well. The dairy barn used only the latest and best farm equipment sold by Sears, including electric milking machines, automatic watering troughs, cement feed troughs with flushing apparatus, and mechanical manure conveyors. Even the dairy barn walls were deluxe, with tile lining the walls instead of the normal whitewash. No expense was spared when it came to farming operations.

The results were impressive. Mr. Loeb's Holstein-Friesian cattle consistently set records for milk production.

1962
Roof of original building Loeb Farms collapses, bringing down hayloft

1963
John VanHaver purchases 100 acres of original Loeb Farms property

1966
JULY 2 – Castle VanHaver opens to public for guided tours and artist gallery

1969
NOVEMBER – Arthur and Erwina Reibel purchase from John VanHaver, plus additional 28 acres, renaming it Castle Farms

1976
JULY 6 – First concert at Castle Farms

1993
Final concert at Castle Farms

1994
Castle Farms sold on Land Contract by Art Reibel to Friends of 4-H

1995
Castle Farms listed on National Registry of Historic Places through Friends of 4-H

Late 90s
Friends of 4-H unable to continue with Land Contract, and property reverts back to Art Reibel

1999
SEPTEMBER – Death of Arthur Reibel

TOP: *Anna and Albert Loeb actively worked the farm.*

MIDDLE: *Purebred pedigree Holstein Friesian bull.*

BOTTOM: *Russell, prize Belgian draft horse.*

He was especially proud of Klorain Marion Finderne, a pedigree Holstein-Friesian dairy cow, who produced thirty five thousand pounds of milk in 1922. The second highest milk producer in the world, Marion needed to be milked four times per day. In addition to the dairy cows and prize-winning Duroc Jersey hogs raised at Loeb Farms, horses played an important part in ensuring the farm's success. With tractors just coming into use, draft horses still pulled their weight in the farming. Anna Loeb herself could often be found up in a wagon, expertly handling the reins. Loeb's prize-winning Belgian horses were housed in the horse barn.

Loeb Farms was a working estate and self-sufficient. An artesian well flowing deep below ground was a convenient source of fresh water for the livestock and various buildings. By 1923, a cheese factory had been established on site. Local dairy farmers were urged to participate in a milk route, with all available milk being shipped daily (except Sundays) to the farm for processing. A large wooden storage tank, lined with heavy sheet tin and bolted to the floor, could handle six thousand pounds of milk, which was weighed as it came in from the wagons. One hundred pounds of milk resulted in eight to ten pounds of cheese. The cheese produced was sold under the name *Golden Leader* through a thriving mail-order business which operated at Loeb Farms.

When it opened to the public, Loeb Farms immediately proved a popular gathering spot. The soaring French chateau towers and majestic stone walls thrilled visitors, who never bypassed an opportunity on Sunday afternoons to stroll the grounds and marvel over the latest farm machinery, view prize-winning registered livestock, or cheer on The Sodbusters, a semi-professional baseball team owned by Mr. Loeb. The Sodbusters regularly took to the field located on the north side of the barn complex. A dugout and stone grandstand were erected across from the Farms' front entrance. Visitors could sit in the bleachers and watch the baseball game while enjoying ice cream purchased at The Cheese Box. During the winter, ice harvested from Lake Charlevoix was brought up Loeb Creek and stored on-site in the Ice House, allowing for tasty frozen treats in summertime. A creek running across the Farm was dammed up, creating an artificial lagoon, which Albert Loeb stocked with swans, ducks, and different types of fancy game.

By 1923, the United States was experiencing boom times; but not so for the farming community. Tariffs earlier put in place by Congress made it difficult for foreign countries to export commodities to the United States. With Americans unable to buy their goods, foreign workers suffered as well. Farmers throughout the United States faced a conundrum: how and where to sell their products? The result was bleak. During the late 1920s, nearly one million American farms went bankrupt.

Many thought Loeb Farms would be immune from the agricultural depression sweeping the nation. After all, Sunday afternoons still saw throngs of visitors strolling the grounds and buying ice cream at The Cheese Box. A local school, Loeb School, funded and constructed by Albert Loeb in 1919, had been built to benefit the community and by 1923 had gained accreditation as a standard school. Life at Loeb Farms seemed an idyllic existence, and while the rest of the country might suffer the calamity of an agricultural depression, residents of Charlevoix had faith that Loeb Farms would be spared. But in October 1924, things abruptly took a turn for the worse with the death of Albert Loeb.

2000

OCTOBER 5 – Linda Mueller purchases 38 acres of Castle Farms at Foreclosure Sale

2001

JANUARY 4 – Linda Mueller finalizes purchase of Castle Farms buildings and property

SUMMER – Linda Mueller works with descendants of the Loeb Family to assure restoration efforts will be authentic and match original blueprints

Clean up, roof, doors, and window repair

2002

Interior of Knights' and Queen's Castles completed

Floors, ceiling, and lighting installed in Knight's Castle

OCTOBER – First wedding held at Castle Farms; Silo roofs rebuilt

2004

Concert stage dismantled and restoration work begins

2004-2005

East and West wings replicated on original footprints; King's Castle completed

2005

Knight's Castle roof salvaged and repaired to original condition

MAY – Linda Mueller's Restoration of Castle Farms completed

Castle Farms opens to public for guided tours

TOP: *Loeb Farms fell into disrepair after the death of Albert Loeb, as shown in the late 1950s, when it was being used for storage.*

BOTTOM LEFT: *Queen's Courtyard overgrown with trees, 1962.*

BOTTOM RIGHT: *Ice house and round office, early 1920s.*

It was common knowledge that Mr. Loeb suffered from ill health and a bad heart, but his passing still proved an unexpected blow to the family. Following his father's death, Ernest Loeb, the second eldest son, was tapped to run the estate. Ernest, trained at Michigan State University, did his best to continue the work begun by his father. Under Ernest's management, the estate expanded its mail-order business to include the sale of cheese, butter, syrup, honey, poultry, and eggs. Trucks from Loeb Farms made daily deliveries.

Ernest quickly earned himself a reputation as an honest and generous employer. He and his wife, Adele, were known for hosting Christmas parties at their home for employees and their families. Ernest himself dressed as Santa and climbed through the window with gifts for all. But business concerns in Illinois also demanded his attention, and his heart and energies became increasingly split.

By 1927, facing the aftermath of an agricultural depression, Ernest called a family meeting. The outcome was not good. The Charlevoix community was devastated to learn that the Loeb Family had decided to close the Farm and sell most of the property, as well as all the livestock and farm equipment. After only ten years, Albert Loeb's dream had died. His beloved Holstein-Friesian cows, the Duroc Jersey hogs, and his Belgian horses were sold at public auction. The mail-order cheese business was purchased by a local competitor. Over the next thirty years, the buildings and remaining property were used solely for storage, and eventually fell into disrepair.

2006

MAY 18 – Linda Mueller presented with Governor's Award for Historic Preservation

Butterfly Garden opens to public

King's West Courtyard Garden opens to public

Knight's Courtyard Garden dedicated to John VanHaver in honor of his restoration efforts in preserving and protecting historic property

2007

Welcome Center opens

Alphabet Garden opens to public

2008

JULY – Castle Farms Garden Railroad opens to public

2009–2011

King's Grand Courtyard Garden and fountain opens to public

2010

SUMMER – Castle Farms Garden Railroad expands to include Fantasy Railway

SUMMER – Reflection Pond Gazebo opens to public

2011

SUMMER – Serenity Garden opens to public

AUTUMN – Purchased 22 acres including part of the Sodbusters' baseball field, bringing the total to 60 acres

2012

Body & Spirit Garden with floor labyrinth, organic vegetables and medicinal herbs

Loeb Farms overgrown and neglected, circa 1962, at the time of John VanHaver's purchase.

YEARS OF CHANGE

CASTLE VANHAVER

Every castle needs its own knight in shining armor. In the 1960s, the great empty stone walls attracted the attention of a dreamer named John VanHaver. A successful business man from Muskegon, Michigan, VanHaver fell in love with the buildings while driving by one day. A talented artist and sculptor with a background in metallurgy and metal casting, he envisioned rescuing the property by creating an artists' mecca with a Renaissance theme. VanHaver contacted the Loeb Family and eventually succeeded in purchasing one hundred acres of the original Loeb Farms property, including the barns, office, blacksmith shop, and manager's house. Renovations promptly began, and the property was renamed Castle VanHaver.

Much work was needed before the first visitors to Castle VanHaver could be welcomed. Time and the elements had ravaged the barns and the roofs in both the East and West wings had collapsed. Clearing away the roof debris was a condition of sale, as well as a top safety priority. Less than a year after purchase, the roof of the dairy barn collapsed, causing further work. Renovations to Castle VanHaver then began in earnest. It was a labor of love that took more than three years. Along the way, VanHaver added a few Renaissance flourishes of his own, including the large Romanesque arch and portcullis at the King's Courtyard Gallery Doorway. A portion of the original horse barn was converted into a foundry for producing original art of cast aluminum.

Castle VanHaver opened to the public for tours on July

TOP: *John VanHaver and friend removing the roof from the area that is now the King's Gallery, 1963.*

BOTTOM LEFT: *John VanHaver showing shipwreck furniture to visitors, 1967.*

BOTTOM RIGHT: *In the area that is now the Queen's Courtyard, John VanHaver sold coffee and pastries for visitors to enjoy.*

2, 1966. Heraldic flags proudly trumpeted the new entrance as visitors thronged to The Castle, thrilled to finally wander the grounds closed to the public for decades. Over the next few years, guests at Castle VanHaver could tour the buildings, plus enjoy a leisurely treat at an onsite coffee shop. A gift shop featured crafts and furniture designed by Van-Haver. An accomplished diver, he dove the waters of both Lake Charlevoix and Lake Michigan, searching for wood from area shipwrecks, which he then fashioned into unique shipwreck furniture. An onsite art gallery showcased Mr. VanHaver's modern paintings, as well as his metal sculptures of heraldic arms, emblems, and escutcheons cast in aluminum and bronze.

During the few years of its existence, Castle VanHaver employed more than twenty people. Just as Albert Loeb before him, VanHaver was respected by his employees, as well as the Charlevoix community. His reputation as a skilled artist grew and much of his original metalwork featuring old English lettering was soon on display all over Charlevoix. Some of it can still be viewed on a few of the downtown buildings today.

A deeply spiritual man, VanHaver considered Sundays sacred. Guests touring the grounds on those days were often treated to the magnificent tenor voice of Mario Lanza crooning the "Our Father" and other spiritual hymns in radio broadcasts soaring high over the stone towers.

VanHaver was, by all accounts, a brilliant man, but by 1969, financial difficulties caused him to rethink his dreams of a Renaissance castle. His eventual decision to sell Castle

VanHaver was made with great reluctance. When Arthur and Erwina Reibel became the third owners in November 1969, they re-named the property Castle Farms.

CASTLE FARMS SUMMER MUSIC THEATER

Erwina Reibel loved horses, and the Reibels purchased VanHaver's property with the intent of founding a riding academy. Although a riding stable was established, new plans evolved, which included a theater and tavern. Eventually, an outdoor concert site was constructed.

As rock music became increasingly popular in the late 1960s and early 1970s, it didn't take long before Castle Farms had earned a name as a premier venue for hosting rock concerts. A fifty-foot wide covered concrete and steel stage greeted concert-goers as they proceeded through a large fenced-in area under the eyes of watchful security guards. After a few years, a grassy earth mound nearly twenty five feet high was built near the road to enclose the view of the stage. Two wings of The Castle were removed to accommodate larger crowds. Reserved seating was installed in the form of wooden benches. Fans with general admission tickets sat on lawn chairs or blankets. Huge amps and immense light towers lit the night sky.

During the next two decades, high energy acts such as Aerosmith, Tina Turner, Ozzy Osbourne, and the Doobie Brothers performed before crowds numbering up to seventeen thousand people. Rock fans were thrilled not having to make the trek five hours south to Detroit or other far-away venues to hear their favorite groups perform.

WHO ROCKED THE CASTLE?

As of 2012, this is who we know Rocked the Castle.

1976
Pavlovs Dog and Nectar . . . . . July 6
Donovan . . . . .August 20

1977
Chicago . . . . .July 6
Jackson Browne . . . . .August 18
The Beach Boys . . . . . . .August 25

1978
The Doobie Brothers . . . . .July 23
Heart and Pablo Cruise . . .August 11
Foreigner & Eddie Money .August 20
Seals and Crofts . . . . . .September 2

1979
Dr. Hook and Jay Ferguson . . .July 6
The Doobie Brothers . . . . .July 22
The Cars . . . . .August 5
Chicago . . . . .August 10

1980
Marshall Tucker Band . . . . .June 22
The Doobie Brothers . . . . .July 4
Alice Cooper & Billy Squier . July 26
Bob Seger . . . . .August 15
The Cars . . . . .August 30
J. Geils . . . . .September 6

1981
Molly Hatchet & The Rockets .May 24
Ted Nugent, Blackfoot &
  Krocus . . . . .June 28
Cheap Trick & Billy Squier . . .July 11
Tom Petty . . . . .July 18
Foghat & Mitch Rider . . .August 16
REO Speedwagon . . . . . .August 22
Chuck Mangione . . . . . .August 29
The Doobie Brothers . .September 5

1982
Ozzy Osbourne . . . . .May 30
Blue Oyster Cult &
  Aldo Nova . . . . .June 25
The Oak Ridge Boys . . . . . .July 17
Rick Springfield & Theatre . .July 30
The Police, English Beat
  & Theatre . . . . .August 15
Heart and John Cougar . . .August 22
Go Gos & A Flock of
  Seagulls . . . . .September 4

1983
Willie Nelson . . . . .July 31
Loverboy & Quiet Riot . . .August 7
Men at Work & INXS . . . .August 23
Def Leppard/Krocus/
  Gary Moore . . . . .August 27
Asia . . . . .September 1

1984
Scorpions . . . . .May 27
Huey Lewis . . . . .June 30
38 Special . . . . .July 12
Frankie Valli . . . . .July 18
Aerosmith . . . . .July 21
Temptations . . . . .August 5
Night Ranger . . . . .August 12
Quiet Riot . . . . .August 25
Billy Idol . . . . .September 1

1985
Iron Maiden . . . . .June 15
Ratt & Poison . . . . .July 4
Pointer Sisters . . . . .July 5
REO Speedwagon . . . . .July 9
Beach Boys . . . . .August 1
Power Station . . . . .August 10
Kenny Loggins . . . . .August 10
Tina Turner . . . . .August 31

1986
ZZ Top . . . . .June 16
Beach Boys . . . . .June 29
Loverboy . . . . .July 15
Stevie Nicks . . . . .July 25
Willie Nelson . . . . .July 28
John Denver . . . . .August 9

1987
Rat & Poison . . . . .June 27
Chicago . . . . .July 4
Bryan Adams . . . . .July 12
Whitesnake . . . . .July 28
Monkees . . . . .August 1
REO Speedwagon . . . . . . .August 8
Huey Lewis . . . . .August 15
Alabama . . . . .August 29
Tina Turner . . . . .September

1988
AC/DC . . . . .May 29
Heart . . . . .July 1
Randy Travis . . . . .July 10
Bob Dylan . . . . .July 13
Whitesnake . . . . .July 16
1st Annual Reggae Festival . . .July 24
Def Leppard . . . . .August 3
Sting . . . . .August 12
David Lee Roth . . . . .August 13
Judas Priest . . . . .August 21
Scorpions . . . . .August 28
Rod Stewart . . . . .September 3

1989
Poison . . . . .May 21
Amy Grant . . . . .July 1
Ozzy Osbourne . . . . .July 7
2nd Ann Reggae Festival . . . .July 30
Beach Boys & Chicago . . . .August 19
Ringo & All Star Band . . .August 20
Bon Jovi . . . . .August 23

1990
Aerosmith . . . . .July 6
Randy Travis . . . . .July 14
3rd Ann Reggae Festival . . . .July 29
Jambalaya Jamboree . . . . . .August 19

1991
Ted Nugent
Def Leppard
Willie Nelson

1992
Moody Blues & Symphony
Marshall Tucker Band
Metallica

1993
Reba McEntire, Lorrie Morgan
Hank Williams, Jr.
The Beach Boys
Kenny G
Marty Stewart & Sammy Kershaw

But others weren't so thrilled. The Castle was often cited for health complaints, noise violations, litter, as well as violation of local zoning ordinances, and many Charlevoix residents weren't happy with the high decibel castle. Since the late 1800s, the quiet little town had gained a reputation as an exclusive summer resort community that catered to the best of families; now Charlevoix was becoming known for huge traffic snarls and a sex-drugs-and-rock'n-roll atmosphere that seemed to invite trouble. With concert fans oftentimes ending up drunk, stoned, and fighting in public, local police were frequent visitors to The Castle. The community breathed a sigh of relief when the last concert was performed in the early 1990s. Sadly, the death of the music seemed to usher in a death knell for the buildings. The Castle fell into a state of disrepair again. Extensive roof and foundation damage occurred during the years of neglect.

In 1994, a local group named Charlevoix County Friends of 4-H made arrangements to purchase fifty acres of the property from Arthur Reibel on a five year land contract. The property was renamed Castle Farms Community Center, and plans were drawn up which would transform it into a countywide youth education center. The stone buildings would house indoor museums, classrooms, and theater. The former cow and horse pastures were perfectly suited for outdoor activities such as soccer and baseball fields, archery, horseback trails and scout camps. The massive stage could also be utilized by hosting concerts featuring classical, folk and jazz music, as well as reggae and blues festivals. While the Friends of 4-H made a valiant struggle to raise the necessary

TOP: *Backstage at the concert stage, where acts would enter, January, 2001.*

BOTTOM: *Aerial view of one of the many concerts held at Castle Farms Music Theatre during the 1970s.*

Photo credit: Photography Plus

monies to purchase the property, ultimately their efforts proved unsuccessful and Castle Farms reverted back to Arthur Reibel. Following his death in 1999, the land and buildings were again put up for sale.

A CASTLE FIT FOR A QUEEN

Linda's fascination with stone architecture began when she was a child growing up in Ohio. Later, she travelled to Charlevoix, Michigan with her high-school sweetheart, Richard Mueller, Jr., whose family had summer ties to the area. Linda had an opportunity to visit the Farms. Even with its roofs in ruins and interior in shambles, the magnificent structures called to her. Years later, with Linda and Richard happily married and still spending summers in Charlevoix, The Castle property came up for sale. Linda prayed for direction. God just seemed to say to her, "Save these buildings." Linda finally had the opportunity to purchase the historic land and stone remains that had captured her heart

so many years before.

"When I was 18 years old, I was fascinated with the great stone walls and arches of The Castle, and I visited it every time it was open for events," Linda recounts. "Now I have an opportunity to restore part of a grand estate, and create new memories for Charlevoix residents and visitors."

Linda Mueller and her husband Richard had just returned from a European vacation when she learned The Castle was for sale. An art historian from Gulfport, Mississippi, Linda's travels with Richard throughout England, France, Germany, Ireland, and Scotland kindled a passion for castles. Discovering that The Castle was available seemed like something out of a fairytale. Linda was determined to rescue the property. Though it took some time, her patience paid off. On January 4, 2001, Linda became the fourth owner of Castle Farms.

It wasn't much of a dream castle. Not only was The Castle's reputation in ruins, major repairs and renovations were needed. Castle Farms, reduced to a thirty-seven acre property, was a public eyesore, with broken windows and crumbling fieldstone walls. Deterioration had set in and the property suffered severely from neglect. The dairy barns and silos were roofless, except for the service wings. The horse barn roof was sagging and near collapse. But Linda was determined to do everything she could to rescue The Castle for future generations.

Shortly after her purchase, Linda hired the Michigan architectural firm of AZD Associates, Inc. Under the direction of architect Kevin Akey, renovations were soon underway. Extensive clean-up and restoration efforts were supervised by Lazer Construction and its owner, Larry Shawn. Sub-contractors were hired from surrounding communities and throughout the State of Michigan to lend their talents in helping save the property. Special attention was paid to protecting both the environment and historic character of the buildings. Whenever possible, materials were restored and original construction details were followed. The concert stage was dismantled and the metal canopy recycled. Of critical importance was restoration of the roofs, doors, and windows. Natural granite fieldstone had to be found. Plans for the project included reconstruction of a missing roof section of the main cattle barn, recreation of the missing cattle barns wings (east and west), and renovation of the horse barn and icehouse. The walls were in remarkably good shape, but some restoration was needed before the 220-foot roof could be built.

Descendents of Albert Loeb still lived on the family estate high above the shore of Lake Charlevoix. His granddaughter, Virginia, who owned "The Big House", was anxious to see what was planned for the barn complex. During the summer of 2001, she contacted Linda. The two of them met, and Virginia was delighted with the restoration. Amazingly, the original blueprints from 1917 were found. Work soon commenced, closely following those designs.

The original roof of what was once the horse barn was saved. The silo roofs were painstakingly reconstructed with original construction details. Well pipes were repaired, flooded basements were drained of standing water, and a major drainage system was installed to prevent future flooding.

After five long years of extensive efforts by Tony Pearsall of W. Pearsall Construction, plus other local carpenters and artisans, renovations were complete. By 2005, The Castle had been restored. Linda's foresight in maintaining the architectural integrity of the great stone walls, the high pitched roofs, French Renaissance towers, and original building techniques resulted in a world-class property of historic significance. Today, Castle Farms is listed on both the State of Michigan and the National Registry of Historic Places.

Linda's devotion to The Castle is evident to everyone she meets. A down-to-earth woman who quietly goes about her

"My husband, Richard, likes to say I got the money from my first husband (him, of course!). We have been very blessed with our franchise in Domino's® Pizza. Richard bought his first store in 1970 at age 21, as soon as he was old enough to sign the contracts and hand over our two years of savings. Over the past 41 years, he has grown the number of stores in partnership with his brother and our oldest son. Most of the profits went into real estate and investments that worked out pretty well. Currently, we have 135 stores, primarily in Mississippi and Louisiana. The first 30 years, I helped him in his business. Then, ten years ago, Richard said it was my turn to pursue my dream, and he has helped me develop The Castle."

life serving God and others, Linda believes she holds The Castle in loving stewardship for Him and future generations. Ultimately, that is her guide.

CASTLE FARMS TODAY

Castle Farms is now open year-round to the public for weddings and receptions, festivals and shows, corporate and social events, plus castle and garden tours. Dramatic towers, soaring stone archways, romantic courtyards and magnificent gardens transport visitors back in time. Perhaps it is most fitting that Castle Farms' distinctive logo embraces the fleur de lis. Long renowned as a mark of French royalty, "fleur de lis" quite literally means "lily flower". The three petals of the lily represent faith, wisdom and chivalry, plus a sign of the divine favor shown on France. Though Castle Farms arose from somewhat less than a noble birth, it has endured—largely due to the faith, wisdom and chivalry of many people committed to the property throughout the years. Linda Mueller's vision to develop a world-class historic property incorporating old world charm and timeless elegance continues to enchant visitors to this day.

TOP LEFT: *Grand Bridal Expo Fashion Show, an annual event in October.*

TOP RIGHT: *Fiber Arts Festival, held annually in conjunction with the Charlevoix Venetian Festival in July.*

BOTTOM LEFT: *Annual Royal Craft Show held every Labor Day week-end.*

BOTTOM RIGHT: *Santa visits the Castle every December.*

All photos this page: Paxton Photography

COMMUNITY LIFE

✦

Throughout the years, Castle Farms—with each of its various owners—as played a distinct and vital role in the life of the Charlevoix community.

Loeb Farms. Sunday afternoons at Loeb Farms provided local residents with a chance to visit the grounds, buy cheese, fresh flowers, ice cream, and cheer on the baseball team.

An avid baseball fan, Albert Loeb formed a baseball team for the farm in 1919. A regular baseball field with stone grandstand bleachers, dug-out, and diamond was erected at Loeb Farms, and the public was invited and encouraged to attend games. In July of 1919, the team squared off against the Charlevoix Amateur League, with proceeds donated to the local hospital. The Loeb Farms team (aptly named The Sodbusters) was part of the Northern Michigan Amateur

Baseball League. The Sodbusters played for a number of years and faced area teams from Boyne City, Central Lake, Harbor Springs, Petoskey, Pellston, Cross Village, and St. Ignace. Mr. Loeb even sponsored an exhibition game between the Chicago White Sox and The Sodbusters. The team disbanded in 1923 after one of its best players, Frank Tubbs, was recruited to play for the Cleveland Indians. Remnants of the old stone bleachers and dugouts that surrounded the baseball diamond are still visible today.

Loeb Farms prize-winning livestock—horses, cattle, and hogs—were featured annually in the Charlevoix County Fair. In 1919, a grand exhibition building was constructed on the fairgrounds by and for the use of Loeb Farms. Committed to bringing better stock to Northern Michigan, Albert Loeb

TOP: *Loeb Farms Sodbusters baseball team, early 1920s.*

BOTTOM: *John VanHaver displaying some of his shields. Some of his metal castings decorated buildings in downtown Charlevoix.*

"The oldest part of Hever Castle dates from 1270. In the late 1400s, the Boleyn family converted the castle into a manor house. It passed to Henry VIII and various later owners. By the 1800s, Hever had fallen into disrepair. In 1903, it was purchased by American businessman William Waldorf Astor, who restored the castle and built the gardens, and a small village behind the castle to add needed space for his family and guests. Since 1983, Hever has been run as a conference center and is open daily for tours. The gardens include a hedge maze, rose gardens, an herb garden, a children's playground, and a formal Italian garden with a walkway and trellis covered in vines and flowers. The Castle Farms buildings were originally built as barns. The dormitory wing was used as a family home for a few years by the third owners, the Reibel Family. For most of its history, Castle Farms has been open to the public and is currently used for weddings, garden tours, proms, conferences and other public events. You can tell from the garden list, I have been taking ideas from Hever Castle: the maze, the rose garden, the herb garden, children's play area and trellis walkway have found places at Castle Farms. I keep looking to Hever Castle for inspiration."

offered many inducements for breeders, and Loeb Farms often played host to meetings of dairymen and breeders, with men of national fame brought in to speak. When Loeb's prize-winning bull Charlevoix Marbury 288868 was awarded the blue ribbon in his class at the 1920 National Dairy Show in Chicago, it earned the animal special merit and won the two-year-old-herd national acclaim. In April 1921, in a show of patriotism with other breeders, Mr. Loeb furnished ten purebred Holstein bulls to be shipped overseas to assist devastated regions of France in their efforts to rebuild and restock in the aftermath of the World War. Albert Loeb took such great pride in his herd of Holstein-Friesian cattle that he registered "Charlevoix" as a trademark name with the Holstein-Friesian Association of America in 1922.

Castle VanHaver. Opened to the public in the 1960s, tourists and locals toured the art gallery and strolled the historic buildings of Castle VanHaver. A gift shop selling VanHaver's original works, plus his shipwreck furniture, was set up in the former cheese factory. Today, shipwreck furniture crafted by John VanHaver can sell for over $10,000. A coffee shop offered refreshments in what is now the Queen's Waiting Room. Guests at Castle VanHaver were able to sit and linger over coffee and snacks at small tables and benches set up amidst the great stone walls and towers of the Queen's Courtyard.

Castle Farms Music Theater. Another type of crowd surged into the Charlevoix community when wild enthusiastic rockers crowded The Castle for open-air concerts. The stage is long gone and some of the rock groups are now disbanded,

"Fortunately, I don't have to do everything myself. As The Castle project expands, wonderful people show up when we need them. I have several departments headed by fantastic people who are very good at their jobs: Weddings, Corporate Events, Tours, House-keeping, Maintenance, Landscaping. Have I missed anyone? We don't have our own kitchens, so we don't have to arrange meals for 150 people one day and 1,200 the next. We have approved caterers who serve great meals at good prices, and they are happy to have the extra business. I have a manager and an assistant manager who do the administrative work. I can focus on what I do best: imagining the next step in creating a world-class historical property. My first love is the gardens. When I have time, you will often find me digging in the dirt and planting flowers."

but for most of the people who attended concerts at The Castle, memories of the music will never die.

Castle Farms. By 2006, Castle Farms had undergone a total historic restoration. Open year-round for tours, The Castle's full-time staff also coordinated weddings, proms, class reunions and corporate events. Visitors from around the world have thronged to The Castle for Renaissance fairs, antique shows, fine art displays, and classic car shows. Eventually, Linda Mueller made a decision to concentrate on weddings, tours, and three annual festivals. Today, Castle Farms is proud to host its Fiber Arts Festival in July, and Royal Craft Show on Labor Day Weekend. Additionally, The Grand Bridal Expo in October includes a wonderful display of antique wedding gowns and quilts from across the decades.

*Castle VanHaver
begins restoration efforts
in the early 1960s.*

ARCHITECTURE

QUEEN'S COURTYARD

This graceful archway is the original entrance to the Loeb Farms complex. Above the smaller arch on the outside of the north wall is a cornerstone bearing the date 1918, the year the dairy barn was built. Workers on the farm drove wagons and equipment under this archway and turned around in the cobblestone courtyard. The south side of the courtyard features a covered arcade, a common design element of castles throughout France. Originally, the five Romanesque arches were enclosed under the dairy barn's enormous roof. Water from an artesian well located under the tavern flows through an ornamental fountain and through an overflow pipe into Loeb Creek. Today, the fountain provides a romantic setting for brides and grooms as they exchange wedding vows.

THE QUEEN'S TOWERS (EAST AND WEST)

Two short towers, known as drum towers because of their short round shape, stand sentry on either side of the archway leading to the Queen's Courtyard. The tower roofs feature the classic "Witch Hat" design prevalent in French architecture. Both towers weathered the years in good repair because they were low to the ground and easy to reach. Much of the original wood was preserved.

THE QUEEN'S EAST TOWER

During the days of Albert Loeb, the east tower was used as a lounge for farm workers. The rest of the wing (known as "The Club") included a

Loeb Farms was designed in 1917 by renowned architect Arthur Huen of Chicago, Illinois. Present day renovations were completed with the assistance of AZD Associates of Bloomfield Hills, Michigan.

TOP: *Cornerstone at Loeb Farms above the second small archway at the original entrance, leading to present day Queen's Courtyard.*

BOTTOM: *Queen's Courtyard with Romanesque arches, leading to a covered walkway.*

kitchen, dining room, locker room, as well as an upstairs dormitory for unmarried farm laborers. Ernest Loeb, second son of Albert Loeb, took over managing the farm after his father's death. Ernest actually lived with the farm workers at The Club during the winter of 1921, prior to completion of his home before his marriage to Adele Fies. In later years, John VanHaver utilized this area as a coffee shop; the upstairs area served as a gallery for modern art. Nowadays, the Queen's East Tower, also known as the Queen's Castle Tower, provides an elegant haven for brides and their families as they await the beginning of the wedding ceremony.

QUEEN'S TAVERN/WEST TOWER

During the days of Albert Loeb, the west drum tower operated as a dairy. Milk processed here was poured into metal milk cans for shipping. The area was sectioned into three separate rooms. One was used for sterilization, one housed the boiler, and the third room contained an area where milking implements were cleaned. The west side of the building featured an outdoor loading dock where milking cans were loaded onto horse-drawn wagons. In 1923, a cheese factory was installed in this area.

Thirty years later, John VanHaver turned the old dairy into a gift shop. His renovations used barn wood salvaged from more than fifty barns throughout Northern Michigan and the Upper Peninsula. The rough hand hewn beams were used to decorate the ceilings. The ruined floor presented a daunting challenge, but under Mr. VanHaver's direction, original tiles were salvaged from the stanchion areas and the

LEFT: *Queen's East Tower was once part of the dairy, where the cheese factory was located.*

BOTTOM: *Restoration of the Queen's bridal wing, 2002.*

Tavern floor was painstakingly created in the exquisite herringbone pattern that can still be seen today. Following his purchase, Art Reibel made further renovations, installing an octagonal dance floor and a bar. Parties replete with swirling disco lights often lasted throughout the night, providing entertainment for invitation-only guests.

Nowadays, the Queen's Tavern offers smaller bridal parties an intimate gathering spot in which to celebrate. The European antique wooden sideboard, with carved lion's heads gracing one wall, was chosen by Linda Mueller from her antique collection to complement this stately room. The sideboard is strikingly similar to one located in Glamis Castle in Scotland, the late Queen Mother's childhood home.

QUEEN'S BRIDAL WING

During the days of Loeb Farms, the downstairs level served as a dining room and kitchen area for farm workers. Eventually, Art Reibel renovated the space into two dressing rooms for concert performers. It has since been remodeled as an elegant bridal suite.

Upstairs, the second level comprised the original dormitory at Loeb Farms. Split into five bedrooms, living quarters were available for up to fifteen farm workers. The dormitory was considered the height of luxury, especially during the winter months. Workers could leave their quarters and head directly to milk the cows, while never having to brave the elements and step outside. Later remodeled by Art Reibel as an apartment, the site eventually became a designated waiting area for concert performers. Look close and you'll spot the name Bon Jovi scratched deep in the surface of a stone.

Today, this area has been renovated into two separate upstairs bridal suites with elegant settees, plus a quiet waiting

The King's Grand Fountain,
designed by Richard Mueller, Jr.

❧

"I love castles and gardens, castle and garden books, and castle and garden magazines. When we travel, I scout out any public gardens along the way. Richard is so supportive, and he takes me to as many gardens as I can find. Then we take lots of pictures and buy books and postcards. I have quite a library. I may be the only person who still looks at guide books 20 years after I bought them. When I am not traveling, I pour over books, magazines and photos, and keep folders of ideas. Every so often, a garden feature will jump out at me and I will have just the right spot to incorporate it into The Castle property."

❧

space on the main floor where brides and their attendants gather before the wedding celebration.

TREASURY

Originally a bathroom adjacent to the farm workers' dormitory, this tiny room was renovated by Art Reibel into something akin to the King's Counting House. During the twenty-plus years The Castle hosted rock concerts, Reibel would retire to this secluded room and count the money garnered through ticket sales. Millions of dollars passed through this room; hence, it has been dubbed The Treasury. Today it serves as an office.

BASEMENT

Fresh water is vital to the success of any agricultural venture and Loeb Farms took full advantage of the artesian well which ran directly under the property. The well, located under the dairy that is now the Queen's Tavern, supplied water to the livestock, as well as the various buildings. Following Linda Mueller's purchase in 2001, over five feet of water and a foot of mud was drained from the dormitory basement area before restoration could begin. The basement now provides much needed storage space for The Castle.

KING'S GRAND COURTYARD

The outside area between the east and west wings was originally fenced in as the barnyard. In later years, a massive outdoor concrete stage with metal roof was erected in this spot. Concert performers could go directly from their dressing rooms and onto stage without being seen. The performers ran through a doorway directly beneath the Romanesque arch John VanHaver had added some years earlier. Wooden benches near the concert stage provided deluxe seating. Concert goers holding general admission tickets had to make do with lawn chairs or blankets on the huge lawn and the surrounding grass berm. The concrete stage was dismantled in 2002. A huge crane managed to remove the metal roof intact in one piece and transported it to a local farm. Ironically, the stage now serves as a shelter for cattle.

Today, the area now known as the King's Grand Courtyard is divided into four sections by sidewalks which intersect near the center. This Courtyard promenade is typical of French Chateau gardens. In the fall of 2009, the courtyard area was extended to include the entire south lawn. This garden was designed on the Renaissance garden principles of perspective and vistas. Trees, shrubs and roses were planted. The King's Grand Courtyard was finally completed in 2010 when four stone maidens representing each of the different seasons were set in place lining the entrance to the Courtyard. A grand central fountain circled by flower beds completes the sweeping vista.

"Richard was back to work at the pizza business after the construction was finished. He understands pizza customers. Twenty- to thirty-year-old brides completely baffle him. He still reviews the financial statements and helps the departments to become more efficient. Last summer, he had a wonderfully creative time adding to the garden railroad. I expect he will think of a few more innovations to entertain kids of all ages. He encourages me to keep developing the gardens, and he adds things himself, like the trout in the pond, the gazebo to watch the fish, and most of the fountains. He loves water features. This past summer we added a new 30-foot diameter fountain in the King's Grand Court that happens to be ideal for remote control boats."

KING'S GREAT HALL AND FOYER

Originally a hay loft for the dairy barn, the King's Great Hall and Foyer covers the entire ground floor. By the time of John VanHaver's purchase in 1962, the roofs of the first floor wings had collapsed; a condition of sale was that VanHaver remove the debris. Other stipulations precluded use of the buildings as dance halls, gambling halls or slaughter houses. The main building's roof collapsed later that year, bringing down the hay loft, but the stone walls remained intact. Nearly one hundred years later, these original walls still exist. They stand as an enduring tribute to the superior craftsmanship of the skilled stone masons who built Loeb Farms.

During the days of Albert Loeb, hay was loaded through large windows in the hay loft from wagons in the courtyard below. It took thirteen pair of Belgian draft horses to accomplish this task. Using photos from the 1920s as a guide in reconstruction efforts, the windows and doors now gracing the King's Great Hall were custom built, including the four large windows with slender French Gothic arches. The two windows at the east and west ends were constructed to match the tall windows found in the Knight's Castle. The floor, ceiling, roof, and lighting were installed during the years of 2004-2005.

KING'S GALLERY

The King's Gallery was originally designed after the galleries of a French Chateaux, where the nobility could promenade and take their exercise during bad weather. At 220 feet long, walking 24 lengths of the gallery adds up to one mile of exercise. During the 1920s, cows paraded

Open House at Castle Farms, 2003, with many of the people who were involved in the restoration.

through the long enclosed hallway of the dairy barn to reach the row of stanchions located here for milking. Loeb Farms had the distinction of being one of the first farms in Michigan to utilize automatic watering troughs and electric milking machines. Albert Loeb's prize-winning cow Kolrain Marion Finderne called this barn home. Years later, the Romanesque arched doorway now gracing the gallery was added by John VanHaver after the roof caved in. Today, completely restored, the King's Gallery offers visitors a glimpse of old-world style in a modern-day setting.

KING'S CASTLE TOWERS

Each end of the King's Castle is guarded by immense round towers, which once held silage for Loeb Farms' two hundred head of cattle. Corn for the silage was grown on the farm, then chopped and loaded into the silos by conveyer. Albert Loeb's commitment to utilize only the finest of innovative farming techniques led him to line the inside of each tower with glazed brick tiles. These tiles, still in place today, were designed to insulate the silage, thereby ensuring fresher and better quality feed for the cattle. The top of each silo tower features decorative stonework, as well as the classic "Witch Hat" design, modeled after castles in France.

The silo tower roofs had not been shingled in many years. Reconstruction efforts meticulously followed architectural aspects of the drum towers found on either end of the Queen's Courtyard. Though it proved more costly, the silo roofs were rebuilt using the original technique of wrapping slender lengths of green poplar wood around supports

"Chenonceau is a manor house castle. The current building was begun in 1515 on the site of an older manor. It is a combination of late Gothic and early French Renaissance styles. The castle had numerous owners over its long history, including six women who each left their mark on the buildings or gardens. In 1913, the Menier family, famous for making chocolates, bought Chenonceau just before WWI began, and they still own it today. In 1951, they began a restoration program of the buildings and gardens to bring it back to its former beauty. Castle Farms shares the late Gothic, early French Renaissance design period. While the 20 x 197-foot gallery of Chenonceau crosses the river, the 28 x 220-foot Castle Farm gallery sits firmly on the ground. The property was bought in 1917 by the Loebs just as the United States entered WWI. Both properties suffered from neglect over time and were later restored and opened to the public."

Sculpture Courtyard at Castle VanHaver, 1967, now the King's Gallery.

tapering to the top. A second layer of poplar wood wrapped in the opposite direction assured a strong foundation for the shingles. Except for the windows, which were lifted into position, the silo roofs were rebuilt in place. Short metal pipes running horizontally up the silo outsides acted as ladders that farm workers used to access the silos; a few of the original pipes still remain.

Today, the towers are used for stairs and elevators.

KING'S EAST AND WEST GARDEN ROOMS

Built to house Albert Loeb's prize-winning dairy cattle, the dairy barn featured two wings, each 42 x 198 feet. Steel stanchions ran down the middle of each wing, with bullpens and pens for calves at the south ends. Some thirty years later, when John VanHaver purchased the property, the roofs on both wings had collapsed and the walls had begun to crumble. Art Reibel removed the entire east wing and all but forty

feet of the west, in order to provide concert goers with a better view of the massive stage he'd constructed between the two wings. Years later, Linda Mueller, determined to restore both wings, contacted the Loeb Family. Amazingly, the original blueprints were still in the Loeb's attic. In 2004, both the east and west dairy wings were replicated on their original footprints, based on plans drafted in 1917 by Arthur Heun, Loeb Farms' original architect. Not knowing how much interior space was needed, the wings stop at 160 feet.

KNIGHT'S CASTLE AND LOFT

During the days of Loeb Farms, the Knight's Castle served as the horse stable. An aisle ran down the center of the room, with stalls on either side housing thirteen pair of draft horses and mules, including Russell, Albert Loeb's prize-winning Belgian draft horse. The stone walls, tall roof with dormer windows, and decorative turrets are all reminiscent of those found in a French Chateau. Gothic arches on the covered porch are similar to those at Amboise Castle located in the Loire Valley of France.

Following Linda Mueller's purchase in 2001, the Knight's Castle was the first building to be renovated. Inside, workers discovered the stone walls were covered by drywall, cement, or had been painted white. Numerous methods were used, including sandblasting the cement. By 2002, the walls had been restored to their original condition. Reinforced cement was poured, colored and stamped to provide a slip-and-stain proof surface that combined ambiance with practicality.

The second floor of the horse stables originally contained a hayloft. Notches above the windows held the ends of the loft's floor joists. Posts from the horse stalls provided additional support. A set of high double French doors allowed workers to load hay into the hayloft from each end. Following his purchase, John VanHaver removed the hayloft in order to accommodate the intense heat rising from his forge and to create more work space. His decision opened the room to a height of twenty-eight feet. In the early 1970s, the building was once again used as a horse stable by the Reibels. Later, after the stage was built, a loft and balcony on the second floor provided Art with a private box for rock concert performances.

In 2001, the Knight's Castle was temporarily converted into a workroom for rebuilding windows and doors. Every door and window on the property was in need of repair. Following this project, the roof situation was addressed, for its

restoration involved serious issues. When the hayloft was removed, much of the roof support disappeared. A variety of traditional architects and engineers were consulted, who all advised that repairs would be too costly and the roof should be replaced. Determined to preserve every historic aspect of the building, Linda eventually found Barn Specialist Dave Ciolek, from the Michigan Barn Preservation Network at Michigan State University along with Architects Bruce and Doris Smith of Pontiac, Michigan. Under Ciolek's direction, winches and jacks were set into place and utilized to slowly pull the roof back into place during a period spanning more than three months. Damaged wood was replaced and new beams and queen style posts were installed where necessary. Nearly the entire original wooden roof was saved. A spiral staircase gracing the east entrance leads upwards to a small loft, which is used for storage.

Today, the Knight's Castle has been completely renovated into a magnificent grand hall where guests at The Castle can dance and dine in a setting fit for a King, Queen or Knight.

KNIGHT'S CARRIAGE HALL

During the 1920s, horse drawn wagons, carriages, and automobiles were stored in the Carriage Hall. Originally, the Carriage Hall was open to the outdoors, on

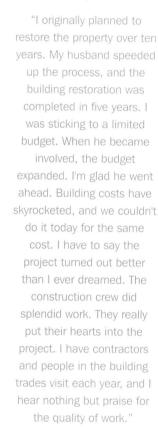

"I originally planned to restore the property over ten years. My husband speeded up the process, and the building restoration was completed in five years. I was sticking to a limited budget. When he became involved, the budget expanded. I'm glad he went ahead. Building costs have skyrocketed, and we couldn't do it today for the same cost. I have to say the project turned out better than I ever dreamed. The construction crew did splendid work. They really put their hearts into the project. I have contractors and people in the building trades visit each year, and I hear nothing but praise for the quality of work."

the front side. The front doors and windows were added in later years. Today, two modern-day carriages are housed in this area. Christmas gifts to Linda Mueller from her brother-in-law and sister-in-law, Glenn and Val Mueller, the carriages—*Prince Charming* and *Lindarella*—were made by the Justin Carriage Co. of Nashville, Michigan, the same company that crafts horse-drawn carriages for use on Mackinac Island.

Grooms hired by Loeb Farms to care for the horses and carriages were quartered above the Carriage Hall. A hallway faced the eastern courtyard. Seven rooms on the west served as bedrooms and one bathroom was shared by all. The Dormitory was eventually converted into modern living quarters and is now a private residence for staff.

Today, the Knight's Carriage Hall is a special area which honors The Castle's second owner, John VanHaver. Several

of his metalsmith pieces are on display.

1918 MUSEUM/BLACKSMITH SHOP

Originally the blacksmith shop at Loeb Farms, the stone foundation for the forge is still intact. Intense heat from glowing coals would have been used to heat horse shoes, which were then pounded and fashioned to fit the horses' hooves. Iron rings used for tethering horses as they were being shod can still be seen fastened in the walls. Though the original floor was probably dirt, the building now features a floor of glazed brick, installed by John VanHaver in the early 1960s with tile he salvaged from the dairy barn.

Following Linda Mueller's renovations, the blacksmith shop was renamed the 1918 Museum in tribute to the era when the farm was built. Historical items featured inside the museum include World War I memorabilia, clothing and

LEFT: *Prince Charming Carriage.*

RIGHT: *Lindarella Carriage.*

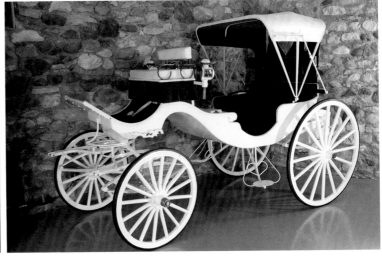

LEFT: *Former blacksmith shop, now the 1918 Museum.*

RIGHT: *Round Office where business was conducted.*

tools, a unique historical mouse trap collection, plus a variety of antique toys available in the 1918 Sears Roebuck catalog. Various artifacts from the days of Loeb Farms unearthed during renovations are also on display in this Museum.

THE CHEESE BOX/STORAGE PAVILION

The Cheese Box was a popular gathering spot in the heyday of Loeb Farms. Dairy products, including cheese, ice cream, flowers, and refreshments were available for sale to the public from this pavilion, which also included a "drive-up" window. Resurrected in the 1970s by Art Reibel, the building was utilized as a concession stand. The consummate entrepreneur, Reibel cooked up the idea of Castle Chicken, which he sold in this location. Today, the Cheese Box provides The Castle with much needed storage space and a place for the Garden Railway engineers to work.

THE ROUND OFFICE

Originally built as an office to manage the daily operation of Loeb Farms, the Round Office has changed very little throughout the years. John VanHaver also used this building as an office from which he directed the renovations and daily management of Castle VanHaver. The Round Office still evokes the simple charm of its construction dating back to 1918. Today, historic photos of the Loeb Family, plus farm records and other memorabilia are showcased in this building. A horseshoe encased within the cement leading up to the porch is part of the original sidewalk.

"Ghosts? There are some unexplained happenings at The Castle, but I don't want to give the impression that it is haunted. They aren't scary things, just unexplained. When something odd happens, we just say "Art did it," referring to the past owner, Art Reibel, who is now deceased."

KNIGHT'S OCTAGONAL TOWER AND LOOKOUT

Known as the Ice House during the time of Albert Loeb, the Octagonal Tower and Lookout might very well have been dubbed Castle Keep (stronghold of The Castle). The decorative arches and buttresses designed by architect Arthur Heun are similar to ones found on castles throughout the French countryside. Crenellations top the Tower walls. In real castles, archers sought cover behind battlements such as these to shield themselves from deadly arrows soaring skyward launched by enemy troops. The Ice House originally boasted an octagonal pyramid roof, as a tribute to the Free Masons (a Fraternal Order to which Albert Loeb belonged).

The door visible along the building's back wall dates to 1918. A second door, long gone, originally faced Loeb Creek. During the winter months, ice harvested from Lake Charlevoix was brought up the creek, hauled through this door and stored in the Ice House to keep food cool during the summer months.

Renovations to the Ice House did not include repair of the roof. Instead, an upper level observation deck was constructed to provide visitors with a panoramic view. One of the large decorative arches was opened in 2005 to provide a dramatic backdrop for romantic outdoor weddings held in the courtyard.

Octagonal tower dressed for a wedding.

"We made a video for tours about eight years ago to explain the history of the property, and Richard and I did some interviews in the video. The past few years when I would introduce myself to visitors, they would occasionally say: 'Was that you? You looked younger in the video.' So, last year I couldn't stand it any longer, and I redid the portions of me speaking. Now guests recognize me right away. I guess the construction aged me faster than my kids did when they were teenagers. Richard looks pretty much the same."

A PEEK INTO THE PAST

ANTIQUE TOY COLLECTION

The Castle's antique toy collection is showcased in the Knight's Carriage Hall. Visitors will discover farm and castle toys ranging from the 19th Century to present day. This collection features dragons galore (though not the fire-breathing kind), plus an entire display case of medieval toy castles and knights jousting at play. Fisher Price® farm toys, plus a variety of cows and horses fashioned from metal and wood, stand alongside dairy wagons, buggies, milk trucks, silos, and John Deere® tractors. And while we've no wish to scare the kids, The Castle's toy bats collection rivals anything seen at Halloween.

1918 MUSEUM COLLECTION PIECES

Artifacts and memorabilia from the era of Loeb Farms are showcased in the 1918 Museum (originally the Blacksmith Shop). A horseshoe found during excavations for the new drainage system is on display, plus assorted nails, hinges, and various hand tools. Many of the items housed in this elaborate collection—including the wooden mousetraps—were sold in the 1918 Sears Roebuck catalog. Other featured items include a collection of old hats, children's board games, and antique toys such as tea party sets, wooden blocks, Kewpie®, and Raggedy Ann® dolls.

When Albert Loeb purchased the property that eventually

TOP LEFT: *1920s French dollhouse, a gift to Linda Mueller from her husband Richard.*

MIDDLE LEFT: *The 1918 Museum contains artifacts from WWI and the 1918 Sears catalog.*

BOTTOM LEFT: *A replica of the Loeb Farms delivery truck.*

TOP RIGHT: *Gong bell toy from the 1918 Sears catalog.*

MIDDLE RIGHT: *Mousetrap collection in the 1918 Museum.*

BOTTOM RIGHT: *Salad bowl made by John VanHaver on display in the Carriage Hall.*

"The Mouse Trap Collection started on a whim. I saw a very interesting mouse trap in an antique store that had a little wheel so the mouse could run around after it was caught. The only kind of trap I knew was the one with a snap bar to kill the mouse. After that, I kept finding more kinds of creative mouse catchers. You know the old saying, "build a better mouse trap and people will beat a path to your door." Who knows? If I display a large selection of mouse traps, it might have the same affect. Leeds Castle (in Kent, England) has a Dog Collar collection. Why not mouse traps? This year, I discovered little racing cars that are powered by mouse traps. The kits have to be assembled, so that should give the maintenance crew a fun job between plumbing problems and peeling paint. I think we can have a lot of fun with mouse trap races at The Castle."

"I began the royal and castle collection in 2002. Some pieces I bought at antique shops. Lately, I have found eBay to be a good source for rare pieces. I have certainly learned a lot about world leaders and the line of succession of royalty through the collections. I love to see parents explain to their children that their family came from a certain country or they visited a particular castle and their memories about it. Occasionally we have foreign visitors, and they are pleased and surprised that I have something from their country. The toy collections began in 1996 when Richard started his antique toy collection. Some of the toys are from Richard's collection. One I really enjoy is the 1918 Sears Catalog collection. I bought a 1918 Sears Catalog because Albert Loeb was an executive of Sears and the property was under construction then. I carry copies of catalog pages with me when we travel, especially to antique toy shows. Some years I find more toys than others. 2010 was a particularly good year for 1918 toys. Children visiting The Castle can see what children in 1918 would have gotten for Christmas. Some of the toys are still around, like Tinker Toys®, trains, dolls, and card games. What is obviously missing are computer games."

KNIGHT'S CARRIAGE HALL COLLECTION OF JOHN VANHAVER

Magnificent examples of the artistry of John VanHaver, The Castle's third owner, are showcased in the Knight's Carriage Hall. The collection includes catapults, knights, crests, heraldic arms, emblems, and escutcheons cast in aluminum and bronze. A gifted metal-smith, VanHaver generously donated many pieces of his work, plus numerous photos from his years of ownership during the 1960s.

HISTORIC WEDDING CAKE TOPPERS

The Main Office Foyer houses Linda Mueller's private collection of historic wedding cake toppers, which date from the late 1800s through present day. A Victorian cake topper under a glass dome features frosting more than one hundred years old. Other bridal memorabilia, including vintage embroidered needlework and antique photos, is showcased

came to be known as Loeb Farms, patriotism was at a fever-pitch. America had officially entered World War I only two months earlier. The 1918 Museum's historic collection includes vintage WWI military and nurse uniforms, bugles, rare children's books, metal toy soldiers, newspaper clippings from the time, and old sheet music such as "After the War Is Over," reminding the soldiers of home.

"The Cake Topper collection started when I saw a magazine article about brides using vintage cake toppers. I still had my cake topper, which my daughter had used on her wedding cake. Then I started buying toppers at antique stores for different decades. My all-time best find is a cake topper that was sold in the 1918 Sears Catalog! The rarest topper is a black couple from the late 1800s. It is in great shape, considering it is made mostly of frosting."

TOP LEFT: *Cake topper from the wedding of Linda and Richard Mueller, Jr., with their wedding party, May 3, 1969. This cake topper was also used at their daughter's wedding in 1996.*

MIDDLE LEFT: *Nicholas and Alexandra of Russia figurine.*

BOTTOM LEFT: *Model of Chamborg Castle.*

TOP RIGHT: *1880s rare cake topper made of spun sugar.*

MIDDLE RIGHT: *King George, father of Queen Elizabeth II.*

BOTTOM RIGHT: *Commemorative plates of castle and royalty.*

"The Royal Collection really took off after I visited Balmoral Castle in Scotland. The Queen Mother had a showcase in the ballroom which is open to the public. It had a collection of royal memorabilia … plates, mugs, cups, and saucers with portraits of each of her family members. So I reasoned, if the Queen Mother thought the display would be interesting to her visitors, my visitors might like them, too. She also had wooden barrel trash receptacles. So I thought, if they were good enough for the Queen Mother, they were certainly appropriate for Castle Farms. I have a very odd collection of castle pictures. Most of my European castle photos show light fixtures, trash cans, restrooms, signs to the restrooms, parking lots, downspouts, drainage ditches, paving materials, benches, and display cases. Whenever I have decisions to make, I just look at what the big castles have. By the way, we have nicer restrooms than many of the castles in Europe."

here. The collection also includes exquisite dolls—Princess Grace of Monaco and Princess Diana of Great Britain—in their wedding gowns, and Tom and Marge Monaghan in honor of their 25th wedding anniversary.

MAIN OFFICE FOYER HISTORIC PHOTO COLLECTION

This vintage black and white photo collection found in the Main Office Foyer dates back to 1917. An exterior shot of the Loeb Family's summer residence showcases architect Arthur Heun's genius and the superior craftsmanship of the stone masons who built the main house and barns. Other photos include construction shots, farm workers, and stable hands gathered alongside tethered horses.

ROYAL COMMEMORATIVE COLLECTION

Linda Mueller's private collection of Royal Commemorative China is on permanent display in the King's Great Hall Foyer and the West Garden Room. A magnificent display of royalty memorabilia celebrates royal families from around the world. Included in the collection are cups, saucers, plates, and other items depicting the crowned heads of Europe (Belgium, Netherlands, Denmark, Sweden, Austria, Norway, Germany, Prussia, France, and Spain), as well as Russia, Japan, and the last Queen of Hawaii. This extensive private collection owned by Linda Mueller also includes Staffordshire®, Royal Doulton®, and Lenox® figurines, vintage needlework celebrating

royal events, and an extensive selection of rare photographs highlighting royalty during World War I. Also of particular interest are the exquisite miniature carriages, the Cinderella® collection, antique toy canons, and replicas of different famous castles throughout the world.

❖

"I keep a life list of castles the way birdwatchers keep a life list: what I spotted, when and where. I currently have over 160 castles, some of which I have seen more than once. They range from empty ruins in fields, to fully furnished and landscaped castles and palaces. The fragmentary ruins are the hardest to identify. I don't count one if I can't figure out what it was. Favorites: Germany: I fell in love with castles when we visited Neuschwanstein in 1986. It was one of the first castles I ever saw. Walt Disney used it as a model for the Disney castles. Even though it was built between 1869 and 1884 with modern construction techniques, it is still awesome. France: I love Chenonceau because it has a very interesting history, and it was owned by six women. My favorite is Madame Dupin, who owned it during the French Revolution. Because she was sympathetic and generous to the villagers, and the castle had the only bridge over the river for miles, her life was spared and the castle escaped destruction. Lesson: If you let people use your castle, they won't chop off your head! England: Hever Castle was the childhood home of Anne Boleyn, second wife of Henry VIII. It is a tiny jewel of a castle. Actually, it was a manor house surrounded by a moat and the gardens are wonderful. I look to that garden often for inspiration."

❖

TOP LEFT: *Harry Potter wizard chess set on display in the Queen's Waiting Room.*

BOTTOM LEFT: *Tickets from some of the concerts held at Castle Farms Music Theatre, donated by concertgoers.*

TOP RIGHT: *Visitors love playing with giant chess game located in the King's Gallery.*

BOTTOM RIGHT: *Reggae Festival held at Castle Farms Music Theatre.*

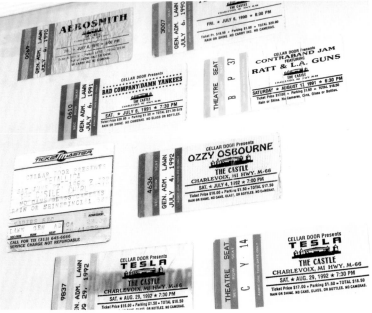

CHESS

The ancient noble game of chess served as the inspiration behind the various rooms found throughout The Castle. Named for pieces on a chess set (the King's Great Hall, the Queen's Tavern, the Knight's Courtyard), the Queen's Waiting Room features Linda Mueller's private collection of chess sets. Guests visiting The Castle can also play a game of gigantic chess with pieces set up in the King's Grand Courtyard or the Gallery in winter. Other outside games, such as bocce ball, badminton, croquet, or lawn bowling, are available for sport in season.

HISTORIC RESTORATION
PHOTO COLLECTION

Visitors touring The Castle will find the Historic Restoration Photo Collection located along a hallway in the King's West Garden Hall. This vast collection documents the restoration process. Thorough photographic documentation proved invaluable for having Loeb Farms barn complex listed as a historic site on both the National and State Historic Registries.

CONCERT MEMORABILIA

Who rocked The Castle? One wall lining the King's West Garden Hallway celebrates the concert years. Posters, ticket stubs, photographs, and other valuable keepsakes make up a permanent display, thanks to the generosity of various people who attended concerts from the 1970s through the early 1990s at Castle Farms.

"I don't plan on having huge concerts while I own Castle Farms. Many people in Charlevoix disliked the concerts because of the noise, traffic, drunk drivers, drugs, and rowdy behavior. I attended one Beach Boys concert in 1986 and enjoyed it immensely. But large concert crowds who have been drinking are impossible to control, and are hard on property and landscaping. Large concerts just aren't part of my mission to serve God and the Charlevoix community."

THE CASTLE FARMS ALBUM QUILT

Hanging high above the showcases in the King's Great Hall Foyer, The Castle Farms Album Quilt was crafted entirely by Linda Mueller's hands. Begun in 2001 following her purchase of the property, Linda completed the quilt in 2006, just as French doors were being installed in the East and West Garden Rooms. The quilt's design illustrates events during the years of The Castle's restoration. Five squares represent the King's, Queen's, and Knight's Castles. The two patriotic stars were fashioned while viewing news coverage of the September 11, 2001 attack on the World Trade Center. The eagle represents God as the center of Linda's life.

CASTLE FARMS ALBUM QUILT

TOP ROW FROM LEFT:

1. King's Castle restored 2003-2006. Original pattern by Linda Mueller.

2. Red Hat Parties, wreath pattern from the Baltimore Album Quilt ca 1850, Linda Mueller private collection.

3. Louisiana Purchase 200th year 1803-2003. Sunflower pattern #41 in honor of Louis XIV, the Sun King. *Papercuts and Plenty*, Elly Sienkiewicz.

4. Flower Urn, in honor of 1st Antique Show (2004) at Castle Farms. Pattern from the Baltimore Album Quilt, Linda Mueller private collection.

5. Queen's Castle restored 2001-2003. Original pattern by Linda Mueller.

SECOND ROW FROM LEFT:

1. Shield for King's Castle. Original pattern by Linda Mueller.

2. Meteor Shower 2003. Linda Mueller was standing in a field by her home in Charlevoix with her mother-in-law, Rosemary Mueller. The sky was cloudy, but about 3:00 am, the clouds parted and they saw 15 meteors in ten minutes. "It was awesome!" says Linda. Fleur de Lis Pattern #62, *Papercuts and Plenty*, Elly Sienkiewicz.

3. Blacksmith Shop restored 2003. Original pattern by Linda Mueller.

4. Charlevoix Petunia Day May 2005. Every year, Charlevoix plants petunias on both sides of Bridge St. at the end of May. Pattern #27 variation: *Papercuts and Plenty*, Elly Sienkiewicz.

5. Shield for Queen's Castle. Original pattern by Linda Mueller.

THIRD ROW FROM LEFT:

1. Star made on 9/11/2001 as Linda Mueller watched the television news. Pierced star appliquéd to background is in honor of those who lost their lives.

2. Butterfly Garden planned 2005 with the Charlevoix Garden Club. Original pattern by Linda Mueller.

3. In God We Trust. God is the center of Linda Mueller's life and the foundation of our country. Original pattern by Linda Mueller.

4. Holly Wreath. Holly Daze fundraiser for the Charlevoix Hospital, held at The Castle since 2005. Pattern #55: *Papercuts and Plenty*, Elly Sienkiewicz.

5. Star made on 9/11/2001 as Linda Mueller watched the television news. Pierced star appliquéd to background is in honor of those who lost their lives.

FOURTH ROW FROM LEFT:

1. Violet basket for Linda Mueller's granddaughter Emma, born in Linda's birth month of February. Pattern #16, Ivy Basket variation: *Dimensional Applique* by Irene Keating.

2. Wedding rings in honor of Anora and Jon Purdy wedding at The Castle October 2002. Original pattern by Linda Mueller.

3. Knight's Castle restored 2001-2003. Original pattern by Linda Mueller.

4. Fleur de Lis, in honor of Pope John Paul II, died April 2005. Pattern #39: *Papercuts and Plenty*, Elly Sienkiewicz.

5. Fall basket in honor of Linda Mueller's grandson Alex born in the month of October. Basket Pattern #23 variation: *Dimensional Applique* by Elly Sienkiewicz.

FIFTH ROW FROM LEFT:

1. Ice House restored in 2004. Original pattern by Linda Mueller.

2. Crown of Laurel in memory of three U.S. Presidents: Ronald Reagan (died 2004), George W. Bush (elected 2004) and Gerald R. Ford (died 2006). Pattern #18: *Baltimore Beauties and Beyond*, Elly Sienkiewicz.

3. Shield for Knight's Castle. Original pattern by Linda Mueller.

4. Lyre and Laurel Spray representing musical events such as the Great Lakes Chamber Orchestra. Pattern #25: *Baltimore Album Quilts I*, Elly Sienkiewicz.

5. Round Office restored 2003. Original pattern by Linda Mueller.

Appliquéd and quilted by Linda Mueller 2001-2006.

TOP LEFT: *Antique bridal gown and quilt collection showing 1830s wedding gown with 1930s quilt on display in the background.*

BOTTOM LEFT: *1920s gowns and quilts.*

TOP RIGHT: *1860 and 1880 gowns.*

BOTTOM RIGHT: *Loeb family wedding gown, on loan from the Loeb family, from 1990s wedding.*

THE STUFF OF WHICH
FAIRYTALES ARE MADE

❧

Once upon a time, a young girl named Anora fell in love with her high school sweetheart. Shortly after graduation in 2000, he proposed. They quickly agreed on a medieval-themed wedding. Soon after their engagement, the young couple was thrilled to learn the Castle Farms property had been put up for sale. How perfect! A wedding at a French Renaissance castle, located in Anora's hometown of Charlevoix. She scoured the newspaper each night, searching for news of who would step forward to rescue The Castle. Anora's persistence was rewarded when an account of the sale was finally printed, listing the name of the new owner: Linda Mueller.

Anora quickly got to work. Tracking down Linda's address, she dashed off a note begging for a chance to host their medieval wedding at Castle Farms. Linda remembers being surprised when she received Anora's letter. A wedding at The Castle? It was 2001 and restoration had barely begun. The property was lined with dusty dirt roads. The buildings were in ruins. Linda put the note aside for some days while she pondered the pros and cons of a wedding at The Castle. Then one day, shortly afterward, Linda's telephone rang. It was Anora, calling to personally plead their case. Linda didn't have the heart to ponder any further. Far be it from her to stand in the way of romance and deny a young girl her dreams. If Anora wanted a wedding at Castle Farms, then Anora would have her wish. Friday, October 18, 2002 was the date chosen for the first wedding at Castle Farms.

While Anora happily started planning her Renaissance-

Fairy tales do come true.

"When we bought The Castle, Richard and I had no clue what would be involved in restoring 70-year-old stone buildings that were in very poor shape, or what we would do with them when we finished. But one of our favorite sayings is, "How hard can this be?" This is often followed with, "What ever made me think I could do this?" And then, "What was I thinking?" The hardest part was to envision how each building would eventually be used, and to engineer in everything that would be needed. We restored first and experimented with uses later. Weddings turned out to be our main business. We have had to go back and rework heating and air conditioning, add catering areas and restrooms, and find more office and storage space as our business expanded. But, for the most part, we did pretty well."

themed wedding, Linda and her construction crew dove into action, focusing their restoration efforts on the Queen's Courtyard, where the wedding was to be held. By October, just days before the wedding, everything including restrooms was completed. The Queen's Courtyard, with its majestic soaring stone towers, had been transformed into an elegant romantic setting like something straight out of a fairy tale. Unfortunately, the weather did not cooperate. When Anora's wedding day dawned, the decision had already been made to move the evening ceremony indoors into the Queen's Tavern.

As guests arrived that cold rainy night, they crossed the paved courtyard to a walk lined with torches lighting the way to the Tavern's door. Anora, dressed in a flowing medieval white gown, made her entrance under an archway of swords to meet her groom, who was garbed in black and white, high leather boots, and a sword at his side. Guests were also invited to dress in costume for the occasion. That evening,

The Castle was bedecked with crusader knights, lords and ladies, yeomen, their goodwives and children, too. Even a court jester was spotted in the party. Everyone agreed The Castle had provided an authentic medieval experience for Anora's wedding. To make the fairytale ending complete, Anora was hired a few months later, and she now serves as Castle Farms' Assistant General Manager.

Since the first Castle wedding on that windy night in October 2002, Castle Farms has provided a romantic setting where, to date, more than six hundred couples have exchanged wedding vows. The Knights Courtyard, The Queen's Courtyard, and The King's West Courtyard feature outdoor wedding sites, while the King's Great Hall includes an indoor chapel. Areas which once housed stable hands and farm workers have been transformed into luxurious rooms for brides and attendants to dress for the ceremony. With a fully trained staff of professional wedding coordinators, Castle Farms offers bridal couples the ultimate in a full serv-

TOP LEFT: *Reception in the King's Great Hall.*

TOP RIGHT: *The Castle's first bride, Anora, enters the Queen's Tavern to meet her waiting groom.*

BOTTOM: *New bride and groom enter Lindarella Carriage for a romantic ride on their wedding day, 2009.*

"In 2003, we had 16 weddings; in 2010, we finished the year with 195 brides, most of whom had their reception at Castle Farms. Word of mouth and the internet are our best sources of advertising. While in much of Michigan business is slow, The Castle wedding business has still managed to grow. Part of that is because people are just becoming aware that The Castle is here. Now that the gardens are maturing, I plan to do more advertising to tourists. The Castle is definitely worth going out of the way to see, and Michigan has so many other wonderful places to visit. The Castle does much more than just tours and weddings. The Tavern is an affordable place to have baby showers, rehearsal dinners, and small parties. Special occasions such as a 90th birthday or a 50th wedding anniversary often take a larger room. Many charities hold events at The Castle, and Castle Farms also has trade shows from time to time. The Castle also has a Fiber Festival and a Royal Craft show in the summer, and Grand Bridal Expo in the fall."

ice wedding venue. To the extent possible, every wish is fulfilled and every effort made to accommodate special requests and all guests' needs.

Coordinators and Castle staff are available to assist with planning, facilitating wedding rehearsals, wedding ceremonies and being present onsite during wedding receptions. Couples choose their own caterers, florists, photographers, cake designers, and other bridal vendors. As Castle Farms does not sell alcohol, couples are free to purchase liquor, beer and wine elsewhere, thereby greatly reducing their cost when served by a licensed bartender. Pre-decorated touches such as hanging ferns, lighted greenery and trees, and draped tulle in magnificent reception rooms enhance the splendor of the original stone architecture. Set-up, teardown and cleaning services are included in all ceremony and reception packages.

Now one of the premiere venues in the Midwest, a wedding at Castle Farms is truly the stuff of which fairytales are made. With beautiful brick courtyards, soaring stone towers, and sweeping gardens, this romantic French Renaissance castle blends old-world charm and modern-elegance for the perfect setting. Best of all, brides are delighted when they discover that a Castle Farms wedding is surprisingly affordable. Free bridal tours are available upon request, including information on room options, availability, and dates. Couples of all faiths are welcome, as well as those who desire a legal non-denominational ceremony. Castle Farms also offers the perfect venue for renewal of vows. To contact a Castle Farms wedding representative, visit our website at www.castlefarms.com and click on the wedding link. You may also phone Castle Farms at (231) 237-0884, or email us at weddings@castlefarms.com.

King's Indoor Chapel provides the setting for an intimate pause between bride, groom and God.

Linda's favorite view from the top of the King's Grand Courtyard.

YOU'RE CLOSER TO GOD'S HEART IN A GARDEN THAN ANYPLACE ELSE ON EARTH

Linda Mueller's passion for castles is rivaled only by her love of gardens. The gardens at Castle Farms—formal and informal—match any of their counterparts found throughout Europe. Drawing on instinct rather than a master plan, Linda's "little sketches" have evolved into stunning works of natural beauty. Through her study of the French gardens of Louis XIV and his landscaper, André Lenôtre, she discovered the thrill of experimenting with different designs. Blending old-world models with a 21st Century approach of sustainable gardening, Linda uses native plants whenever possible, as they are less labor intensive and more suited to the environment. She considers the Castle Farms gardens to be a particular blessing from God, who loves gardens, just as He does weddings, families, and people having peaceful days.

THE MAIN FOUNTAIN GARDEN

The Main Fountain Garden area has seen numerous changes. Originally a grassy circle near the parking lot, this beautiful informal garden eventually grew to include ornate stone benches that surround a swirling sidewalk. This colorful spot, always abloom with seasonal flowers such as daffodils, dahlias, petunias, mums, ornamental grasses, and shrubs, showcases the grand formal fountain that welcomes visitors to Castle Farms.

THE HERB GARDEN

Found outside The Enchanted Forest, The Castle's Herb Garden transports Castle guests back to days of yore, as sweet scents of French tarragon, summer savory, germander, tansy, calendula, oregano, borage, and basil fill the air.

An antique European fountain greets visitors as they approach the Castle.

✦

"There are so many times during a person's day when they're hassled or when they're rushed. Things aren't going well. It's nice just to get a breather, to get a little beauty and peace in your soul. A lot of people say it's very peaceful here, and formal gardens typically are very peaceful, very stable, very orderly. A lot of people don't have that in their lives—stability, peace, and order. So, even though it's not currently in fashion, people need tranquility and order."

✦

LEFT: *A spring view of the East Garden with lavender.*

RIGHT: *King's Grand Courtyard under construction, 2009.*

This lovely lyrical garden also includes parsley, sage, rosemary, and thyme.

THE EAST GARDEN

The East Garden holds the distinction of being the second oldest garden at Castle Farms. Designed by Linda Mueller to honor the virtue of femininity, fragrant flowers bearing women's names such as lilies, lavender, roses, daisies, pansies, veronica, petunias, hyacinth, and iris grace the East Garden. Other flowers such as daffodils, Russian sage, Allium, Columbine, Lamb's Ear, and cat mint have since been added, producing constant bloom in the East Garden. Graced with morning sunshine, garden chairs, and a beautiful fountain, the East Garden was inspired by a French castle garden to be a quiet spot where visitors may enjoy a moment's respite from the hectic pace of modern-day life.

THE KING'S GRAND COURTYARD GARDEN

Ground broke on the King's Grand Courtyard Garden in late autumn 2009; work continued throughout the season in 2010, and was completed in 2011. This gorgeous Renaissance garden with its lawns, garden, and fountain, is based on the splendid landscaping found at Chambord Castle in France. The King's Grand Courtyard Garden features a multi-terraced vista set amidst fragrant roses, amalanchor, viburnum, and yew hedge. Four dazzling maidens carved of stone, each portraying one of the four seasons, grace the courtyard and greet Castle guests as they make a grand promenade through this splendid parterre. At the bottom of the steps, the French Garden Gazebo ensures exquisite photos. With a flowing fountain as the crowning centerpiece, the King's Grand Courtyard Garden offers guests a majestic setting and sweeping vista of The Castle grounds. Linda and her husband Richard often can be found sitting on the stone

TOP: *Queen's Rose Garden features a variety of nearly thornless roses.*

BOTTOM: *Butterfly Garden features butterfly chairs.*

bench at the top of the hillside, holding hands and taking in the view. It is Linda's favorite spot at The Castle.

THE QUEEN'S GARDEN

Begun in 2004, the Queen's Garden is one of The Castle's oldest and most beautiful gardens. Overflowing with fragrant nearly-thornless roses, this beautiful spot also features Rose-of-Sharon shrubs, as well as dianthus and spring tulips. The thornless rose bushes line a lovely sitting area where visitors can enjoy the simple splendor and peace found in this elegant yet informal garden.

THE BUTTERFLY GARDEN

Created in 2006, the Butterfly Garden is an exquisite secluded area popular for smaller outdoor weddings. The boxwood hedges offer complete privacy, and the distinctive butterfly chairs are a fanciful touch to this beautiful setting.

Colorful annuals, including butterfly bushes, hydrangea trees, lavender, daisies, delphinium, and columbine fill the garden with delightful fragrances. Butterflies abound in this pretty little setting. Guests with sharp eyes may also catch a glimpse of a passageway which leads to a secret courtyard.

THE CHILDREN'S GARDENS

The Alphabet Garden. Children love reciting their ABCs in the Alphabet Garden. Designed in 2007, this pretty little garden runs along the north side of the Hedge Maze. With whimsical painted figures and colorful signs, the Alphabet Garden features flowers ranging throughout the entire alphabet, from Astilbe through Zinnia.

The Hedge Maze. For fun and fantasy, schedule a stop at

"Most of my fun stories are on me. I like to talk to visitors, answer questions and make them feel welcome at The Castle. I don't always introduce who I am. One of our visitors stopped in the gift shop on the way out and remarked that we have the friendliest gardener. Peggy, who is in charge of the gift shop, laughed and said, 'You must have met the owner.'"

The Alphabet Garden.

TOP LEFT: *A village scene from the Castle Farms Garden Railroad.*

MIDDLE LEFT: *Observation towers overlook the Train Gardens.*

BOTTOM LEFT: *The Fantasy Railroad features whimsical trains and fairy gardens.*

RIGHT: *The Tornado Tower, designed by Richard Mueller, Jr.*

All photos this page: Paxton Photography

The Castle Hedge Maze, part of The Castle Train Garden(s). Train tracks swoop overhead as guests enter or leave the Maze through one of the three entrances or exits. Inside the Maze, small stone statutes such as a swift sure-footed hare and slow-moving tortoise race through twists and turns.

The Castle Garden Railroad. Model trains have always played a special role in The Castle's history. Ernest Loeb and his older brother, Allen, were train aficionados. Even as adults, both brothers spent considerable time working on train lay-outs. At Christmas time, Ernest splurged on elaborate Lionel train sets for his three daughters. More track was added every year, filling up the living room. During the holidays, Ernest and Allen would host a "train party" for their friends and children, who naturally were excited to begin playing with their trains. But as the tracks had to be manually switched with "Y" switches, Ernest and Allen always got involved and eventually took over. Each year, the children ended up as spectators rather than being able to enjoy playing with their new train cars.

Just like the Loeb brothers so long ago, Richard Mueller, Jr. and his brother, Glenn, share a love for model trains. Richard and Glenn's creativity in track layouts and scenery eventually culminated in The Castle Model Garden Railroad. Opened in 2008, it immediately proved a favorite spot for children of all ages. The 2010 Fantasy Railroad expansion nearly doubled The Castle's Garden Railroad size, easily making it one of the largest working model garden railroads in Michigan. Over 50 G-scale trains operating on seven separate levels zip across more than two thousand feet of track. The trains are easily viewed from eye level or the Victorian tower bridge.

The original Garden Railway depicts scenes of Charlevoix from the 1860s through the 1960s, including a replica of the historic Charlevoix railroad swing bridge, the Charlevoix train depot and the Charlevoix red lighthouse. The Fantasy Railway steams its way through the Hedge Maze and features a fantasy theme. Included in the Fantasy Railway is a 26-foot-long bridge, the Double Helix Tornado Tower and the Five Level Twin Coaster. A 2011 addition of a Lionel train room inside one of the Victorian towers expanded the Garden Railroad to include seven operational trains steaming across two levels of track spanning more than 100 feet in length.

THE KING'S WEST GARDEN

Created in 2006, this elegant formal garden immediately proved a popular outdoor location for brides. The graceful white garden gazebo was designed by a Loeb family member. Magnificent arborvitae line the West Garden fence. The West Garden blooms with flowers including Annabelle hydrangeas, dianthus (which were known during the French Renaissance as "gilliflowers"), snapdragons, white day lilies and other annuals.

"My husband and his brother, Glenn, played with trains when they were growing up. Glenn liked the scenery, Richard liked complicated track lay-outs. When they both became grandfathers, they decided it was time to get back into model trains. This time they decided to try outdoor garden scale trains. Glenn wanted scenery. Richard wanted complicated track lay-outs. You can tell who designed which of the two train areas. They have a wonderful time working on the trains when they are in Charlevoix each summer. The maintenance crew and landscapers have fun, too, even if it involves long hours to get finished for the next train event."

LEFT: *The West Garden Gazebo.*

RIGHT: *The Trellis Walkway.*

LEFT: *Circular flowerbeds adorn the driveway leading to the Knight's Castle and Courtyard.*

RIGHT: *Linda Mueller with John VanHaver in 2006.*

THE TRELLIS WALK

Opened in 2009, this open trellis walkway is designed after the covered walkway found at Anne Boleyn's childhood home of Hever Castle near Kent, England. Hydrangeas and wisteria wind their way up the sides and across the roof. The Trellis Walk is a fragrant covered walkway that provides the perfect photo opportunity for bridal couples before or after they exchange wedding vows.

THE KNIGHT'S COURTYARD GARDEN, DEDICATED TO JOHN VANHAVER

Part of the original stable grounds of Loeb Farms, this beautiful secluded garden bordered by hedges was the first Castle garden to be completed by Linda Mueller. Colorful daffodils, tulips, holly hocks, lavender, bleeding hearts, begonias, coreopsis and iris abound, but the Knight's Courtyard Garden is most renowned for its thornless roses: Zephrine Drouin, with its sweet sensual fragrance; and Kathleen Harrop, developed in 1919 (the era The Castle was built).

Kiss a frog and he'll turn into a prince? This garden also features a Prince Charming frog fountain (originally a horse trough) which flows continuously. The Knight's Courtyard Garden was dedicated to John VanHaver in 2006, in recognition of his foresight for preserving the property as a castle, as well as a historic landmark.

TOP: *Sid the Sea Serpent, given to the Castle by Richard Mueller, Jr.'s brother Glen, stands guard over the Reflection Pond.*

BOTTOM LEFT: *The Reflection Pond gazebo where visitors can enjoy a shady spot to sit a spell and feed the fish.*

BOTTOM RIGHT: *Frog fountain in the Knight's Courtyard.*

"My future plans are to keep developing the gardens and expand the gardens in the south lawn area. I have a tentative plan drawn, but it will likely change as I go. I have a hard time staying with one plan; new ideas come all the time. I am also working with a horticulturist to enlarge our composting program. I am so excited about compost and have used it in my garden at home for years. The Castle project takes it to a new level."

THE REFLECTION POND

Bordered by day lilies, the Reflection Pond is an idyllic setting for guests visiting The Castle. Stocked with large rainbow trout, the Reflection Pond is guarded on the south side by Sid the Sea Serpent. Gracing the east shore is a charming garden gazebo which was designed and built in 2010. With three sheltered swings on which to relax, the gazebo is a perfect spot for feeding the ducks and fish, or simply relaxing and enjoying the view.

THE SERENITY GARDEN

Completed in 2011, this scenic shady spot is accessed by crossing a whimsical bridge over a bubbling brook. The Castle's Serenity Garden is a peaceful little setting off the beaten track. Visitors will find benches and chairs where they can sit and chat, or simply dream the day away.

THE ENCHANTED FOREST

A whimsical wooden sign points the way to The Enchanted Forest, one of the most magical spots in all The Castle grounds. Children of all ages delight in playing hide-and-seek with the fairies and gnomes dwelling beneath the bushes and trees, visiting the North/South pole, or near the criss-crossing bridges and strolling twisting paths. A natural area for local flora and fauna, native flowers such as wild asters, lady slippers, and joe pie weed thrive in the Enchanted Forest. Quail, rabbits, birds, voles, and porcupine have also been spotted, guarded by a Mossy Moose.

LEFT: *The Serenity Garden, a peaceful, shady spot.*

MIDDLE: *Playful brownies greet visitors as they enter the Enchanted Forest.*

RIGHT: *The Mossy Moose in the Enchanted Forest.*

is for Allum
and Aster

2012
ALPHABET GARDEN
FLOWERS

is for Bellflower

is for Cosmos
and Cranesbill

is for Dragonhead
and Delphinium

is for Echinacea

is for Fennel

is for Germander

is for Hens and
Chicks, and Hyssop

is for Iris "Boo"

is for Jacob's Ladder

is for Kale

is for Lamb's Ears

is for Marigold,
Mallow and
Money Plant

is for Nasturtium

is for Obedient Plant

is for Pincushion
Flower

is for Queen
Anne's Lace

is for Rose
Baby Love

is for Sneezeweed
and Sea Holly

is for Twisted Grass

is for Umbrella Palm

is for Violet

is for Wand Flower

is for Xeranthemum

is for Yarrow

is for Zinnia

THE FUTURE FOR CASTLE FARMS

What does the future hold for Castle Farms? Certainly more gardens, more brides, and more visitors. Thanks to Linda Mueller's vision, Castle Farms is now a world-class historic property and wedding venue. Green areas abound throughout The Castle grounds, embracing nature and all its beauty. Linda's love for The Castle continues, as does her commitment to the property and the surrounding community. Intent on refining and beautifying her evolving vision, The Castle remains her one true legacy.

As to what the future holds for this majestic estate once known as Loeb Farms, and now Castle Farms, there is inspiration and foresight in Linda's own words: "The future will be looking back at what we are creating today."

Fond of telling guests she wishes for The Castle to eventually be known as "The Happiest Castle in the World," Linda's visionary approach in restoring the historical site and buildings has resulted in a magical place that appeals to young and old alike. Today, where cows and horses once roamed, romantic courtyards with soaring arches offer bridal couples an intimate spot to exchange wedding vows. Visitors of all ages delight in touring the great stone buildings, wandering the magnificent sweeping gardens, marveling over the trains at The Castle Model Garden Railroad, playing a leisurely game of giant chess, and feeding the ducks and rainbow trout found in the Reflection Pond. Thanks to Linda's vision, Castle Farms offers guests a glimpse into a world long forgotten, where old-world charm and timeless elegance blend in perfect harmony and the happy echo of children's laughter mingles with the soft rustle of satin, lace, and tulle. Throughout The Castle walls and amid the beautifully manicured lawns and gardens, smiling friendly faces abound.

The Happiest Castle in the World. Linda's wish for The Castle is coming true.

The Castle glows at night.

HERE AND THERE

❦

Inspiration falls within the realm of the dreamer. From designs of long-ago to modern day marvels,
it's our hope you find it interesting to browse this section of "Here and There."

World War I destruction of French chateau, 1918.

Castle Farms in ruins when purchased in 2001.

Amboise Castle, a medieval Gothic fortress in the Loire Valley of France, features a series of distinctive Romanesque arches designed by the French King Louis XII. Note the similarity in style to the arches lining the interior of the Queen's Courtyard.

The **Castle of Rothenburg**, Germany, with two turrets on both sides of its Rodertor to guard off intruders, Rothenburg Castle's turrets and entrance bear a striking resemblance to the graceful curves of the archway at the Queen's Courtyard, the original entrance to Loeb Farms.

The **Yew Maze at Hever Castle**, the English manor childhood home of Anne Boleyn (second wife of Henry VIII) is a formal garden designed in the early 1900s by William Waldorf Astor in the Renaissance style. Arborvitae in The Castle's Hedge Maze surround the Fantasy Railroad and each year the trees grow taller. Soon they'll rival the eight foot tall yews found at Hever Castle.

Chambord Castle, in the Loire Valley of France, was originally built by Francois I in 1519 as a hunting lodge. Its world-famous horseshoe-shaped formal French garden served as the inspiration for The King's Grand Courtyard Garden.

Chapel of **Usse Castle** in France.
Loeb Farms' octagon-shaped Ice House.

THEN AND NOW

This pictorial history of "Then and Now" offers a fascinating glimpse into the past and present, gracing the peaceful pastoral setting of Loeb Farms to the fully restored buildings and grounds open to guests at Castle Farms today.

A long **milking parlor** in 1918 lined what is now The King's Gallery. By 1982, the roof had collapsed. (Note the section of massive concert stage in the upper right hand corner of the photo) Nowadays, The King's Gallery serves as an indoor chapel in the event of rain and during the winter months.

The **Barn Interiors** were filled with milking stanchions for Albert Loeb's 200 head of Holstein Friesian dairy cows. Today, the West Garden Room serves as an elegant reception hall for bridal couples and their guests.

The **original entrance** to Castle Farms included a separate drive which forked to the right, for pick-up at the Cheese Factory. The second driveway is long gone, and today the entrance is a stunning entrance to the Queen's Courtyard, The Castle's most popular outdoor bridal venue.

The **Farm Manager's Office** had changed little throughout the years. Today it serves as a little museum of its own, tucked away in the seclusion of the Knight's Courtyard.

The **Blacksmith Shop**, **Horse Barn** and **Carriage House** serviced and housed transportation equipment and animals at Loeb Farms. Today, the area is a popular outdoor bridal venue.

The **East Milking Parlor** grounds directly adjacent to the building needed extensive underground repair before Linda Mueller's restoration work could begin. Today, guests enjoy the quiet simplicity found in the elegant East Garden.

The **original Silo Tower** roofs and walls were crumbling and in danger of collapse. Linda Mueller's vision resulted in complete restoration of the towers, plus a stunning glorious garden known as The Butterfly Garden.

The **Queen's Courtyard** was in desperate need of restoration after years of neglect. Linda Mueller's construction crew worked diligently to make sure this popular outdoor bridal venue was fit for royalty.

The **Cow Pasture** fell into ruin after Loeb Farms closed. Castle VanHaver opened to the public on July 2, 1966, with heraldic flags flying at the entrance. Today the driveway and main entrance has been transformed into a sweeping vista known as The King's Grand Courtyard.

Loeb Farms was a popular spot for people to visit on Sunday afternoons. Today, the soaring stone towers of the King's Castle welcome visitors entering from the west.

The **Queen's Tavern** was nearly in ruins at the time John VanHaver purchased the property. His restoration of the Drum Tower roof and herringbone floor salvaged from original stone glazed tile have resulted in a stunning setting perfect for intimate gatherings.

The **Concert Stage** erected by Arthur Reibel in the 1970s was a massive structure where various musical groups performed. The stage was dismantled following Linda Mueller's purchase and the area turned into a peaceful outdoor courtyard.

King's Grand Courtyard Garden, from concept to completion.

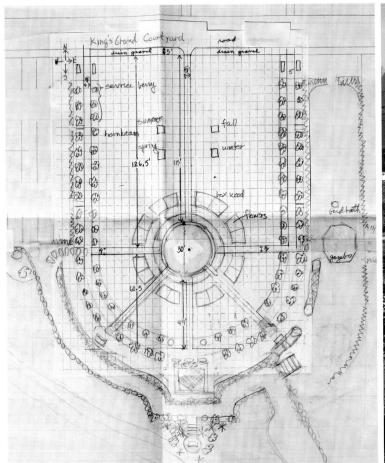

OWNERS

ALBERT LOEB, OWNER OF LOEB FARMS

Albert Henry Loeb

Albert Henry Loeb was born on February 18, 1868, in Rockford, Illinois. The son of Moritz and Johanna Loeb, he was educated in Chicago public schools, and attended Johns Hopkins University. He married Anna Bolmen of Chicago, Illinois on April 26, 1894 and their family grew to include four sons: Allan, Ernest, Richard, and Thomas. Mr. Loeb taught public school while attending law school and was admitted to the Illinois State Bar in 1889. Following his admittance, Loeb and a former law school classmate formed a firm under the name of Loeb and Adler, where he practiced law until 1901 when a business opportunity with Sears, Roebuck & Company presented itself. Initially hired to serve as Secretary of the Corporation, Mr. Loeb eventually was named Treasurer and Vice-President of Sears. During World War I, Loeb was called upon to serve as the company's acting President. In 1917, his decision to invest in more than 1,600 acres of prime Northern Michigan real estate on the shores of Lake Charlevoix led to the creation of a majestic summer residence. Close by, the working model dairy farm (known as Loeb Farms) showcased farm equipment sold in the Sears catalog. Albert Loeb died from heart complications in October 1924.

Hired by Albert Loeb was Arthur Heun, a renowned architect with Michigan roots. A contemporary of Frank Lloyd Wright, Heun began his architectural practice in 1893 with an office in Chicago. His designs quickly caught the interest of wealthy entrepreneurs of the time, such as Charles B. Pike, Joseph Bowen, and William McCormick of Blair Astor Street. Heun's fame led him to design many stately Illinois landmarks, including mansions such as Mellody Farms (the Armour Estate in Lake Forest), the Meeker Estate (Arcadia Farm, Lake Forest), the Loeb family home in the Hyde Park-Kenwood region, the Casino Club (1914), plus palatial estates in Highland Park, including the Ravinia compound for Julius Rosenberg (President of Sears & Roebuck), and a stately mansion for Ernest Loeb, the second son of Albert and Anna Loeb. Born in Michigan, Heun spent the majority of his life working in the Chicago area. Through his long-time association with Albert Loeb, Heun soon became an intimate acquaintance of the Loebs. Fondly known by family members as "Uncle Arthur," Heun even had his own bedroom at the Loeb's summer residence in Charlevoix. Arthur Heun passed away in June 1946.

JOHN VANHAVER, OWNER OF CASTLE VANHAVER FROM 1962 – 1969

John VanHaver

Born in the early 1900s, John VanHaver was a successful businessman from Muskegon, Michigan who rose to prominence as Vice President of the Foundry Division of the Sealed Power Corporation. A famed bodybuilder who was once a finalist in the Mr. America contest, John VanHaver was also a talented artist and sculptor with a background in metallurgy and metal casting. Never married, and with no children of his own, his dreams took the form of leaving behind the corporate life to create a vista for craftsmen and visitors to embrace artistic ventures. In 1962, during a visit to Northern Michigan, VanHaver happened upon the Loeb Farms property. Envisioning an artists' mecca with a Renaissance theme, he contacted the Loeb family and convinced them to sell one hundred acres, including the original Loeb barns. Restorations soon began and the property re-opened in 1966 as Castle VanHaver. For three years, guests flocked to tour the grounds, strolled beneath the soaring stone towers and browsed the shops displaying artistic works, including VanHaver's original creations of metal sculptures, heraldic arms, emblems, and escutcheons cast in aluminum and bronze. In 2006, the Knight's Courtyard Garden was dedicated to John VanHaver in recognition of his fore-sight in preserving the property as a castle, as well as a historic landmark. Today, John VanHaver resides in Grand Rapids, Michigan. His legacy endures.

ARTHUR REIBEL, OWNER OF CASTLE FARMS FROM 1969 – 1999

Arthur Reibel

Arthur Reibel was born on February 16, 1933 in Michigan, the son of Joseph and Helen Reibel. Upon graduation from the University of Detroit Law School, he married Erwina Bell. Reibel eventually became a partner in the law firm of Reibel, Oliver, Dinan in Troy. In 1968, he and his wife moved to Charlevoix with their two daughters, Kimberly and Steffani. During his lifetime, Reibel embarked on a variety of careers. He served as a Great Lakes captain on tugboats, a Certified Public Accountant, Charlevoix County District Court Judge, as well as a corporate auditor with the Internal Revenue Service. In 1969, Arthur and Erwina purchased Castle VanHaver with the intent of establishing a riding academy, theater and tavern. Eventually, an outdoor concert site was established and the venue was renamed Castle Farms. During the years 1976-1993, more than 100 different bands rocked The Castle. Reibel died in September 1999.

LINDA MUELLER, OWNER OF CASTLE FARMS FROM 2001 – PRESENT

Linda and Richard Mueller, Jr.

Linda Mueller was born February 9, 1949 to Don and Eva Holliday of Sandusky, Michigan. Her parents later moved their family to Lakewood, Ohio, where Linda attended public school and met Richard Mueller, Jr., her high school sweetheart. It was while visiting Richard's family at their summer home in Charlevoix that Linda first saw Castle Farms (then Castle Van-Haver). She and Richard toured the property, and Linda fell in love. Following graduation, Linda enrolled at Kent State University to pursue a study of art, but romance intervened. Linda left school and married Richard on May 3, 1969. While Richard was busy working to grow a business called Domino's Pizza®, Linda was busy raising their family of four children: Richard III, Kathy, Chris, and Mike. And while Linda enjoyed being actively involved in family life and helping Richard design each of his new pizza restaurants, she never forgot her passion for art, her love of history, and the majestic castles she'd toured while visiting Europe. At age 52, she began her own career in historic preservation and garden design. Today, thanks to Linda Mueller's vision, Castle Farms has been restored to its original splendor.

CASTLE FARMS AWARDS

1995, "Loeb Farms Barn Complex" officially listed with the National Register of Historic Places, certified by the State Historic Preservation Office (as presented by the National Park Service, U.S. Department of Interior, November 29, 1995). This prestigious listing, as authorized by the National Historic Preservation Act of 1966, denotes historic American places worthy of preservation.

2006, The Governor's Award for Historic Preservation is presented to Linda and Richard Mueller, Jr. Then Governor of Michigan, Jennifer Granholm, cites the Muellers for their "collaboration and commitment to excellence for historic preservation." This high honor is bestowed upon those "… committed to transforming historic structures into vital economic assets … and inspiring to preserve historic buildings."

2006, M Award, Excellence in Masonry Design (presented by Masonry Institute of Michigan and AIA Michigan) award presented to Castle Farms. The M Award seeks to honor works of distinction and outstanding buildings and projects designed by Michigan architects.

2006, Charlevoix Chamber of Commerce Ambassador Award presented to Linda Mueller. This annual award is given to individuals who actively seek to promote the spirit of the Charlevoix community and Chamber.

2007, Margaret Duerr Book Award presented to Linda Mueller. This prestigious award from the Charlevoix Public Library is presented annually to a deserving individual who demonstrates "… a special interest in the quality of life in Northern Michigan."

2008, Best of Weddings, Upper Midwest, presented to Castle Farms by *The Knot*, nationally renowned for its award-winning wedding website, books, and magazines.

2008, Crème de la Crème Best of the Best Wedding Award, presented to Castle Farms by Wedding Merchant's Business Academy, a nationally renowned company "dedicated to the business side of the wedding business."

Soaring stone towers guard the Butterfly Garden on a snowy winter's day.

2008, President's Award, presented to Castle Farms by Keep Michigan Beautiful, for efforts "substantially contributing to … beautification, site restoration and historical preservation."

2009, Charlevoix Area Garden Club Inspirational Award presented to Castle Farms, for beautification efforts.

2009, Business of the Year, presented to Castle Farms by Charlevoix Chamber of Commerce, for its "inspiration to others and … vision … demonstrating success and exceptional performance in business practices, customer service and community involvement."

2009, Best of Weddings, Upper Midwest, presented to Castle Farms by *The Knot*, nationally renowned for its award-winning wedding website, books, and magazines.

2009, Barn of the Year, presented to Castle Farms by Michigan Barn Preservation Network. This esteemed non-profit agency annually honors heritage barns within the State of Michigan, combining integrity and originality in preservation efforts

2011, Best of Weddings, Upper Midwest, presented to Castle Farms by *The Knot*, nationally renowned for its award-winning wedding website, books, and magazines.

CHARLEVOIX THE BEAUTIFUL

✦

There's a reason it's known as *"Charlevoix the Beautiful."* This renowned summer resort community in Northwest Lower Michigan combines small-town friendliness and Up-North appeal in a picturesque setting. You'll know you've arrived when you spot the petunias! These perky little blooms line Charlevoix's famous four-mile long stretch of petunia beds which escorts you into the downtown area, a charming three-block region overlooking Round Lake (often cited as the best natural harbor on Lake Michigan).

Downtown Charlevoix features an exclusive shopping area. Open year round, the unique boutiques, galleries and bookshops cater to guests. Doors are often open well past 10 pm or later, depending on when the last visitor walks out the door. Then, of course, there's "the bridge", an easy stroll at the end of downtown. Opening on the hour and half-hour for the colorful sailboats and huge yachts entering Charlevoix's stunning Round Lake Harbor, this quaint drawbridge built in 1949 is a perennial family favorite.

Indulge your sweet tooth while watching the sailboats with an old-fashioned ice cream cone. Park benches in East Park beckon visitors to sit and enjoy the view of the yacht

Downtown Charlevoix.

A panoramic view of Castle Farms looking toward Lake Charlevoix.

basin. During the summer season, the grassy haven of East Park is the place to be. Tuesday nights, the Charlevoix City Band takes to the stage in the Odmark Music Pavilion. On Thursday evenings, the Pavilion plays host to the Charlevoix Summer Concert Series. Charlevoix's spectacular new City Marina, directly in front of East Park, is the perfect place to spend an evening. This beautiful new marina, home to spectacular sailboats and enormous yachts cruising Charlevoix's beautiful harbor and Round Lake, also features the East Park Trout Habitat, designed with a Northern Michigan trout stream in mind, and the Fountain of Youth. This 30' heated interactive water fountain with choreographed lighting and music delights children of all ages. An easy stroll through the soft summer night along the Pine River Channel brings you to Charlevoix's famous South Pier Lighthouse. It's the perfect spot for viewing the million dollar sunset as it sinks behind Lake Michigan... the perfect end to the perfect evening.

Charlevoix is situated on three beautiful lakes. Crystal blue waters beckon visitors to enjoy all kinds of water activities. Sailboats, jet skis, and kayaks are readily available for hire. Chartered boats from local marinas provide easy access to Lake Michigan, where the fish are always biting. Feel like relaxing in the sun? Charlevoix is famous for its beautiful public sandy beaches. They're perfect for swimming or strolling, as you hunt along the shores, searching for the elusive Petoskey Stone, the state stone of Michigan. Golfers will find a gem in any of the area courses, including a municipal nine-hole course, or the historic Belvedere Club, founded in 1925, and home to the Michigan Amateur State

Championship on 39 occasions. Feel like stretching your legs and taking a bike ride? The Little Traverse Wheelway is a beautiful stretch of scenery. Beginning just north of Charlevoix, it winds its way along the sparkling waters of Lake Michigan on a 26-mile paved pathway perfect for biking, roller blading, running, or any other form of non-motorized travel. Hiking enthusiasts will also enjoy Mt. McSauba, a fifty acre natural recreation complex owned by the City of Charlevoix, featuring wooded hills, steep sand dunes and a pristine shoreline.

History buffs will also enjoy Charlevoix the Beautiful. The Harsha House Museum, a Victorian beauty located one block from downtown, is owned and operated by the Charlevoix Historical Society, and offers a fascinating glimpse into Charlevoix's past. The museum features an extensive collection of photos, antiques, collections from the area, including Ernest Hemingway's wedding license. Hemingway grew up spending his summers in the Charlevoix region. Some of his Nick Adams stories are based on the Charlevoix area.

Another famous Charlevoix resident, Earl Young, was married to Irene Harsha, whose family built the Harsha House in 1891. Young, who lived most of his life in Charlevoix, was a renowned architect who learned the art of working with stone from the skilled masons who built Castle Farms. Earl Young's architectural designs, fashioned of Onaway stone, eventually earned him international acclaim. Built as private residences in the 1950s, these whimsical little homes resemble miniature mushrooms sprung from the

ground. Visitors delight in the drive-by tour of the famous Mushroom Houses, uniquely Charlevoix.

Charlevoix the Beautiful is a year-round resort area. The Charlevoix Venetian Festival during the third week of July is a week-long celebration featuring family friendly activities, carnival, two spectacular firework displays, and a moonlight boat parade on Round Lake. Both Charlevoix's Waterfront Art Fair and Craft Show, held during the summer months, attract juried artisans to East Park. Castle Farms' Fiber Arts Festival (July), and Royal Craft Show (Labor Day weekend) add to the festivities, and The Castle's Annual Grand Bridal Expo in October is not-to-be-missed! Apple Fest, held in East Park during October, regularly draws visitors to the region as produce from local orchards and renowned crafters from around the state display their wares for one final blast of fall fun. Winter sports enthusiasts love the downhill skiing and groomed cross-country trails found at Mt. McSauba.

For more information about the numerous activities Charlevoix the Beautiful has to offer, please contact the Charlevoix Chamber of Commerce, the Charlevoix Convention and Visitors Bureau, or visit either of their websites for up-to-date information on area events.

We look forward to welcoming you!